MW00511430

JESUS AND THE GOSPEL TIMELINE

BOOK II

THE 8 DAYS OF HOLY WEEK

As reported in

The Gospels of

Mark

Matthew

Luke

John

BY

EARL C. DAVID

Intermedia Publishing Group

THE 8 DAYS OF HOLY WEEK

Published by:
Intermedia Publishing Group, Inc.
P.O. Box 2825
Peoria, Arizona 85380
www.intermediapub.com

ISBN 978-1-935529-73-6

Preface

Most of the so called contradictions in the Gospels may be simply insufficient evidence at our present disposal. Case in point; until the work on the Dead Sea Scrolls was released we did not know how to interpret the differing comments of Mark, Matthew, and John at the meal with Simon the Leper.

The statement, "You cannot understand the four Gospels until you know the Fifth Gospel," is absolutely true. *The 8 Days of Holy Week* confirms this truth in many places through the commentary.

The 8 Days of Holy Week is anything but a conventional study of the Gospels. It helps seekers, new converts, and seasoned Christians avoid confusion and misunderstanding when reading and studying the Gospels as separate entities.

The basic premise of *The 8 Days of Holy Week* is everything in God's creation occurs on His timeline within a given context and has a beginning, middle, and end.

The goal of *The 8 Days of Holy Week* is to establish as accurately as possible the timeline of Jesus' last week of human life as reported by Mark, Matthew, Luke, and John. Since no one gospel provides this information per se, I have connected the points of information found within the four Gospels to establish the timeline.

The birth stories are found in the opening chapters of Matthew and Luke. Each Gospel closes with their unique version of Holy Week. Obviously, the Gospel writers were not concerned about stating exactly where and when Jesus spoke or healed. Occasionally they tell us it was morning, evening, or at a particular location but this was not of great importance to them. It was of the greatest importance for them to preserve what they considered the most important sayings, acts, and events in Jesus' life and this they did in an impeccable fashion.

Almost every study of the Gospels is centered on a particular book with some references to the other three. When references are given the reader must turn to other Gospels and search them out. For most readers the outcome results in a significant degree of confusion. The repetition of the parables, teachings, healings, and special events can become a giant puzzle with too many pieces.

The 8 Days of Holy Week contains every word of all four Gospels related to the events of Holy Week. *The 8 Days of Holy Week* offers a new approach to reading and studying the Holy Week. When the subject of the text is found in more than one Gospel all are presented on the basis of date written, for example, Mark, Matthew, Luke and John. *The 8 Days of Holy Week* moves with a compelling story line from the meal at the home of Martha, Mary and Lazarus to the ascension thus establishing the timeline of all the events contained in the four Gospels.

It is also worth remembering that chapters and verses were added to the text hundreds of years after the entire Bible had become the acknowledged book of faith for the Christian community.

Acknowledgements

To Elizabeth, my wife and soul mate who listened to all of my frustrations and victories and maintained the courage to tell me the truth without any sugar coating. Without her I may have never finished this "labor of love."

Jim Ross, author of two books, who took time from his writing to read and offer clarity and sincere interest in my work, and his wife Lucy. Mike and Joyce Haggard for their willingness to proof read and offer so many helpful "considerations." To Mike Willis who has read these pages almost as many times as I have and who is teaching it to his Sunday School Class.

I am deeply grateful to Dr. Donald Strobe who shared with me his amazingly clear and concise depiction of Israel's early history and geography and his permission to use it in this work. I want to say a special thanks to David Longworth for his unselfish sharing with me and permission to use his discourse on the Garden Tomb. Special thanks to Deborah Murdock who has patiently guided me through my legal questions. This work would never have been done except for John Uran whose computer skills have paved a way for me to use this wonderful invention.

I simply cannot say enough about the adult students who made time in their busy schedules to become a focus group. They listened as I taught the lessons in *The 8 Days of Holy Week* and engaged me as they raised questions and helped me make more clarity in the book.

I am deeply indebted to my good friend and the best guide in Israel, David Aaron. David has brought my "Spiritual homeland" to life in a vibrant way.

Without all of you this book would never have become a book.
Thanks
Rev. Earl

Table of Contents

Sunday was a day of momentous importance. A series of questions develop amid the divergence in the reporting. How many meals at Bethany are we talking about? Who poured the costly ointment? Did all the Inner-Circle become angered? Or was it only one? Who was plotting to kill Jesus and Lazarus? Who got up and walked away filled with anger? Why was he so angry?

Modern day Palm Sunday actually occurred on Monday of Holy Week. Before entering the city Jesus was moved to tears. There are differing accounts of Jesus' entry into the city that require exploration. John stated that many authorities believed in him. Jesus did not remain in Jerusalem overnight.

As Jesus neared the city he saw a fig tree. The events surrounding this tree will continue for the next several days. Jesus was very busy on this day. Among the things that occupied his time were the Temple authorities who challenged Jesus' authority; he taught with many parables, and when he reminded them of the stone rejected by the builder many became intensely angry. When Jesus exited the city he went to the Mount of Olives to spend the night.

Chapter 4
Holy Week: Wednesday Morning

The First day of the feast of Unleavened Bread is more easily understood when we know there were two calendars operative at this point in time. More Gospel material is dedicated to this day than any other portion of the story of Jesus.

Jesus resumed teaching in the Temple. The Pharisees and Herodians team up to discredit Jesus but fail. Then the Sadducees attempt to discredit Jesus and also fail. The Scribes (Lawyers) were next to try discrediting Jesus but faired no better.

Jesus then blistered his critics saying, "Woe unto you Scribes and Pharisees, hypocrites blind guides who can swallow a camel before seeing what is right!" At last they sought cover as Jesus called them whitewashed tombs, and a brood of vipers.

Chapter 5
Holy Week: Wednesday Afternoon

Wednesday afternoon Jesus left the Temple and returned to the slopes of the Mount of Olives. Sitting with the Inner-Circle Jesus began to tell them about many things: the end times, the tribulation, and the great desolating sacrilege that would come to Jerusalem. He challenged them to remain faithful because no one, including himself, knew when these things would come.

Chapter 6
Holy Week: Wednesday Evening - The Last Supper

Jesus returned with the Inner-Circle to the Essene quarter to celebrate his last Passover meal. His hour had come! Unlike our favorite paintings of the Last Supper the fact is they were lounging Roman style around a Triclinium. The events in the Upper Room would lead Judas to leave before the final blessing.

In the tradition of the great men of God Jesus delivered his farewell address to these, his closest friends. Jesus closed with a prayer saying, Holy Father, keep them in thy name keep them from the evil one, I pray for those who believe through their words.

Gethsemane

After singing a hymn Jesus and the eleven left the Upper Room and
exited the city. They traveled through the Kidron Valley and ascended
the slops of the Mount of Olives making their way to the Garden of
Gethsemane. Along the way he warned them they would all fall away
before the night was over. Inside the garden Jesus ordered eight of the
disciples to remain at a certain place while he and the big three went
further. Jesus was deeply troubled and asked all of them to remain
awake and pray. Three times he arose from his prayers to find all of
them asleep.

The Arrest

The third time Jesus awoke the disciples he announced the hour was
upon them. Judas appeared leading a contingent of armed men to
arrest Jesus.

The Religious Trial

Jesus was taken first to Annas, the father-in-law of the High Priest,
Caiaphas. After some questioning Annas sent Jesus on to the High
Priest. Peter followed at a distance. There was another disciple present
too. The unnamed disciple had access to Jesus' interrogation. Peter
could go no further than the courtyard where Jesus' words came true
culminating with the crowing of the cock. The unnamed disciple came
to Peter's comfort. Witnesses were called to testify against Jesus. The
questioning came to an end as the beating of Jesus began.

Chapter 8   *page 145*
Holy Week: Thursday - Day of Trials

Very early Thursday morning Jesus' religious trial continued. Caiaphas
held sway over the Sanhedrin and needed the death verdict to come
from his arch enemy Pilate. One of the most overlooked verses in the
Bible concerning Judas hanging himself occurred when they began to
transfer Jesus to Pilate. What do we really know about Judas?

Jesus was taken to Pilate for the political trial to begin. The Jews did
not enter the Praetorium because it was a place of Gentiles and they
did not want to be ceremonially unclean at Passover. Pilate saw no

reason to get involved. The religious authorities immediately brought forth more charges against Jesus. Pilate's first verdict was that no crime against Rome had been committed. When Pilate learned that Jesus was a Galilean he sent him to Herod Antipas. Failing to get what he wanted from Jesus Herod Antipas turned him over to his guards who beat him and returned him to Pilate.

Once more Pilate found no fault in Jesus and tried to release him. In the end he had Jesus scourged.

Chapter 9 *page 165*
Holy Week: Friday - Day of Crucifixion

Pilate tried for the last time to release Jesus. It was now approaching mid-day (explanation of the relationship of calculating time in the Gospels to present day calculations). Pilate washed his hands and released Barabbas.

Jesus was scourged again before being delivered to be crucified. Simon of Cyre'ne was compelled to carry Jesus' cross part of the way. The crowd followed to the hill called Golgotha. (The process of crucifying is described here). Two others were crucified at the same time. The verbal abuse began almost at once. The religious leaders ridiculed him and then the soldiers followed by many others. The only compassionate voice that day belonged to Jesus. One of the criminals believed in him and said so.

Mary watched everything with the agony only a loving parent can experience. When Jesus gave up his Spirit the curtain in the Temple was split from top to bottom, the earth quaked, and the centurion believed. Joseph of Arimathea was a member of the Sanhedrin, very wealthy, and a believer. He was granted permission to take Jesus and bury him.

Chapter 10 *page 193*
Holy Week: Saturday / Sabbath

Day of rest for most of the nation, but for a small hand full of desperate men it was a day of more plotting.

What was this first Easter Sunday like? John's account varies from the others and includes the napkin. Matthew tells us about the guards reporting to the authorities. Luke gave us the account of the events on the road to Emmaus.

During the first Easter day Jesus appeared to the Inner-Circle, now numbering eleven, but Thomas was not present. Later Thomas sees Jesus and believes.

Jesus' time on earth was rapidly coming to a close. The Inner-Circle was in danger of falling apart when Peter announced he was going fishing. At dawn the fishermen were surprised to see Jesus had already prepared their breakfast. After the meal Jesus took Peter for a walk along the shoreline and a little talk.

The Ascension accounts according to Mark and Luke differ in some ways. John closes the Gospel narratives with his own personal witness.

Sample page

This is a sample page to illustrate the most valuable way to read and study, *The 8 Days of Holy Week.*

This column will always contain the passage to be studied. Here is an example: **Six days before Passover** (Passage heading) **John 12:1-2** (Text to be examined) A single reference means this information is found only in the Gospel cited. If there is more than one Gospel that contains a similar account the Book and Passage will be cited. The order of citation will be: Mark, Matthew, Luke, or John. This ordering is based on the earliest writing to the last.	This column will always contain the commentary associated to the passage.

Comments beneath the columns appear at the points where valuable information is given to help enlighten the passage from sources other than the Bible. These can also be personal comments by the author.

Chapter 1

Sunday before Holy Week

Comment

Divergence in the reporting

Most commentators work from the premise that the stories concerning the meals at Bethany are actually the same meal with unexplained major differences. I will briefly mention the issue.

The differences between Mark, Matthew, Luke, and John have long been a point of controversy within the Christian church. Some have interpreted this as an out and out contradiction. Others have tried various ways to reconcile the two positions without harming either.

The first difference concerns the number of days from the meal to Passover.

Father Pixner's approach reconciles the difference based on the Essene calendar and the priestly calendar. From the Dead Sea Scrolls we have learned of the existence of these two calendars and that they were both operative during the days of Jesus.

Father Pixner explains it this way:

Mark 14:1-3; *Now the Passover ... two days away...*

Matthew 26:1-7; *... he said to his disciples: Passover is two days away...*

Luke makes no comment concerning the number of days.

John reports: *Six days before the Passover...*

Father Pixner resolves the difference between the counting of the days until Passover saying, "We may tentatively assume that the dinner in Bethany was given on Sunday. In Mark and Matthew we count:

Sunday plus two days (Monday and Tuesday), that brings us to the eve of Wednesday, the Essene Passover. In John we count six days: Sunday, Monday, Tuesday, Wednesday, Thursday, Friday and we come to the Sabbath, on which, in the year 30, the Temple Passover was celebrated."

The second divergence concerns in whose home was the meal served?

On this difference most commentators seen to ignore all consideration that there could have been two meals given in Bethany. Father Pixner's position, being more logical than most, still postulates only one meal being under consideration.

I believe there is another explanation that meets all of the needs without harming any passage of Scripture. When Jesus returned to Bethany, on his way to Jerusalem, he paused to visit his friends Mary, Martha and Lazarus. Lazarus and his sisters prepared a meal and invited Jesus to be the guest of honor. This meal took place on Sunday, six days before Passover. The second meal in Bethany took place four days later in the home of Simon the Leper.

Six days before Passover	*Six days before Passover*
John 12:1-2 1 Six days before the Passover, Jesus came to Bethany, where Laz'arus was, whom Jesus had raised from the dead. 2 There they made him a supper; Martha served, and Laz'arus was one of those at table with him.	**John 12:1-2** ***Mary Martha Lazarus*** **Comment** The brother Lazarus and his two sisters Martha and Mary were apparently celibates. In Israel, celibacy was considered a virtue only for Essenes, and later for some segments of Christianity. Jesus, a celibate himself, liked to be the guest of Lazarus and his sisters in Bethany. In light of the Essene presence in Bethany, many events now become clearer to us.

Meal number 1

There is no doubt John is reporting a meal that took place in the home of Lazarus, whom Jesus had recently raised from the dead; Martha and Mary were present.

Bethany

All four Evangelists agree Bethany was the location for these events prior to Jesus' entry into Jerusalem. Since Bethany, near Jerusalem, played an important role during Jesus' last days in Judea, it deserves a closer look. Built on a limestone ridge, sloping to the south, Bethany was located less than two miles from Jerusalem.

In his writings about the Temple Scroll (11 Q MIQDASH, 46,16 to 47,5) the famed archaeologist and Qumran researcher Yigael Yadin expressed his conviction that Bethany was one of the three villages, mentioned in the Temple Scroll, that were located east of Jerusalem in which Essene lepers and those afflicted with other impurities were allowed to settle. Because of their uncleanliness, such people were not permitted to enter Jerusalem, and especially not allowed into the Temple compound. Leviticus 13:45-46 says, "*the person with such an infectious disease ... must live alone; he must live outside the camp.*"

Bethany's location east of Jerusalem, on the slope of the Mount of Olives overlooked the Temple district. For those refused entry into the city and Temple much solace was gained from being able to view their beauty from this vantage point. How fittingly that Mark tells us Jesus ate in the home of Simon the Leper.

According to the Jewish writers, Philo and Flavius Josephus (BELL JUD. 2,124), Essenes lived in most of the towns and villages of the Holy Land. Bethany could have been significantly influenced by the Essene theology.

Mary anoints Jesus' feet

John 12:3
Mary took a pound of costly ointment of pure nard and anointed the feet of Jesus and wiped his feet with her hair; and the house was filled with the fragrance of the ointment.

Mary anoints Jesus' feet

John 12:3

Comment
John unequivocally named Mary as the one who anointed Jesus' feet. She anointed his feet with an expensive fragrant ointment of pure nard.

Mary then dried his feet with her hair. Women seldom if ever cut their hair in Jesus' day. In order for her to dry his feet with her hair she "had to let it down," To let down one's hair in public or in the presence of a man other than her husband meant she was breaking a cultural taboo.

And the priest shall set the woman before the LORD, and unbind the hair of the woman's head, and place in her hands the cereal offering of remembrance, which is the cereal offering of jealousy. And in his hand the priest shall have the water of bitterness that brings the curse. - Numbers 5:18

Luke relates a similar story of yet another meal in a different time, context, and with a different host but with the same use of the woman's hair to dry Jesus' feet.
(Ref. Luke 7:36-50).

Nard

"This hardy herb, nard, is a member of the Valerianaceae family, grows in the foothills of the Himalayas. The part of the plant growing underground has the appearance of a fibrous spindle, and is rich in the precious essential oil. From India, nard was transported in the form of a dry rhizome or oil phase extract, via Persia, under the name nardin. Nard has an intense, warm, fragrant, musky note, similar to the aromas of humus. It exhibits a wide range of fragrances among the root-type perfumes." Source: Wikipedia.

We can better appreciate the value of the nard when we realize that it was grown in the Himalaya Mountains of India. It was then transported through the land of Persia and into the Holy Land and beyond. The very fact of harvest and transportation would impact the cost significantly.

Plotting to kill Jesus and Lazarus	*Plotting to kill Jesus and Lazarus*
Luke 22:1-2; **Mark 14:1b-2;** **Matthew 26:3-5**	**Luke 22:1-2;** **Mark 14:1b-2;** **Matthew 26:3-5**
Luke 22:1-2	**Comment**
1 Now the feast of Unleavened Bread drew near, which is called the Passover. 2 And the chief priests and the scribes were seeking how to put him to death; for they feared the people.	All four Evangelists agree that a plot to kill Jesus was decided upon. They also agreed the plot must be sprung after the feast not during the celebration. Matthew said this meeting took place at the palace of Caiaphas, the High Priest. John alone stated that they also intended to kill Lazarus.
Mark 14:1b-2	
1 And the chief priests and the scribes were seeking how to arrest him by stealth, and kill him; 2 for they said, "Not during the feast, less there be a tumult of the people."	

Matthew 26:3-5
3 Then the chief priests and the elders of the people gathered in the palace of the high priest, who was called Ca'iaphas, 4 and took counsel together in order to arrest Jesus by stealth and kill him. 5 But they said, "Not during the feast, lest there be a tumult among the people."

Crowd gathers to Jesus and Lazarus

John 12:9-10
9 When the great crowd of the Jews learned that he was there, they came, not only on account of Jesus but also to see Laz'arus, whom he had raised from the dead. 10 So the chief priests planned to put Laz'arus also to death.

Crowd gathers to Jesus and Lazarus

John 12:9-10

Comment
Word spread that Jesus was in Bethany and people came from far and wide to see him and Lazarus. The raising of Lazarus had aroused a renewed hope that the Anointed One was in their midst.

The crowd had no idea that the chief priest was planning to put both Lazarus and Jesus to death. This point is frequently overlooked.

Four Days Later

Four days later the meal at Simon the leper's took place. Both meals took place in the town of Bethany but on separate days and with separate attending circumstances. Jesus celebrated his Passover meal on Wednesday evening in the Upper Room. Since then most people have referred to it as the "The Last Supper." The Orthodox would celebrate their Passover meal on Friday evening.

Two days until Passover

Mark 14:1a;
Matthew 26:6

Mark 14:1a
It was now two days before the Passover and the feast of Unleavened Bread.

Matthew 26:1-2
1 When Jesus had finished all these sayings, he said to his disciples, 2 "You know that after two days the Passover is coming, and the Son of man will be delivered up to be crucified."

Two days until Passover

Mark 14:1a;
Matthew 26:6

Comment
Four days later the meal at Simon the leper's took place.

The meals at Bethany serve as our prelude to the beginning of Holy Week.

Bethany and Simon the Leper

Mark 14:3a;
Matthew 26:6

Mark 14:3a
And while he was at Bethany in the house of Simon the leper,

Matthew 26:6
Now when Jesus was at Bethany in the house of Simon the leper,

Bethany and Simon the Leper

Mark 14:3a;
Matthew 26:6

Comment
It is probable that Simon's leprosy had been healed by Jesus and he was no longer considered contagious. The evidence of the disease may have still remained and would have made it impossible for him to worship in the Temple. This was the reason he lived in Bethany, a village of the Essenes'.

Simon the Leper

Simon had been healed, but he still wore the marks of his illness in the form of scar tissue. These scars made him ceremoniously unclean, because they represented his previous condition. Any thought of entering the temple was absolutely beyond the most remote of possibilities. The next best thing for him was to go to the brow of the Mount of Olives where he could look down upon the beautiful city of Jerusalem and the magnificent Temple. One can only imagine the amount of joy that this provided for those forbidden entry to both Jerusalem and the Temple.

The issue of "Unclean"

Uncleanness was a social / religious taboo related mainly to health issues. Most of us would be unclean according to the code [Leviticus 21:16-20].

16And the LORD said to Moses, 17Say to Aaron, None of your descendants throughout their generations who has a blemish may approach to offer the bread of his God. 18 For no one who has a blemish shall draw near, a man blind or lame, or one who has a mutilated face or a limb too long, 19 or a man who has an injured foot or an injured hand, 20 or a hunchback, or a dwarf, or a man with a defect in his sight or an itching disease or scabs or crushed testicles;

Healing the "Unclean"

Most of Jesus' healings were for people declared unclean. The Law observing Jews tried to avoid dealing with those called unclean. The "unclean" included lepers, prostitutes, cripples, those who were uncircumcised, and those possessed. One memorable example of Jesus' compassion for the unclean was his encounter with a man possessed by many demons whose name was Legion. Jesus cast out the unclean demons of Legion, allowing them to enter the forbidden "swine!" Jesus believed no person made in God's image should be treated as unclean.

Luke tells us (Luke 17:11-19) Jesus entered a Samaritan village where he was met by a wandering band of ten lepers. It would not have been an uncommon thing to find such a group of lepers wandering together. They were prohibited from approaching people regarded as clean. They were required to call out "unclean, unclean" as they approached another person.

Instead of crying out unclean, they cried out, "Jesus heal us." Jesus' instantaneous response was "Go and show yourself to the priest." This very statement means he had healed them.

Show yourself to the priest

When Jesus said, "Show yourself to the priest" he was referring to Leviticus chapter 14.

1 The LORD said to Moses, 2 "This shall be the law of the leper for the day of his cleansing. He shall be brought to the priest; 3 and the priest shall go out of the camp, and the priest shall make an examination. Then, if the leprous disease is healed in the leper, 4 the priest shall command them to take for him who is to be cleansed two living clean birds and cedarwood and scarlet stuff and hyssop; 5 and the priest shall command them to kill one of the birds in an earthen vessel over running water. 6 He shall take the living bird with the cedarwood and the scarlet stuff and the hyssop, and dip them and the living bird in the blood of the bird that was killed over the running water; 7 and he shall sprinkle it seven times upon him who is to be cleansed of leprosy; then he shall pronounce him clean, and shall let the living bird go into the open field. 8 And he who is to be cleansed shall wash his clothes, and shave off all his hair, and bathe himself in water, and he shall be clean; and after that he shall come into the camp, but shall dwell outside his tent seven days. 9 And on the seventh day he shall shave all his hair off his head; he shall shave off his beard and his eyebrows, all his hair. Then he shall wash his clothes, and bathe his body in water, and he shall be clean." - Leviticus 14:1-9

It is important to note Jesus never hesitated to touch a person called "unclean."

Woman anoints Jesus' head	*Woman anoints Jesus' head*
Mark 14:3b; **Matthew 26:7**	**Mark 14:3b;** **Matthew 26:7**
Mark 14:3b As he sat at table, a woman came with an alabaster flask of ointment of pure nard, very costly, and she broke the flask and poured it over his head.	**Comment** Earlier translations do not use the word "table" but the concept of the word carried the meaning of everything for the meal was furnished "at the table."
Matthew 26:7 a woman came up to him with an alabaster flask of very expensive ointment, and she poured it on his head, as he sat at table.	Mark and Matthew report a woman came with an alabaster flask of ointment to anoint Jesus. "The 'alabaster' of the Bible, is often termed *Oriental alabaster*, since the early examples came from the Far East. This 'Oriental' alabaster was highly esteemed for making small perfume bottles or ointment vases called alabastra, and this has been conjectured to be a possible source of the name. Calcite alabaster is either a stalagmitic deposit, from the floor and walls of limestone caverns, or a kind of travertine, similarly deposited in springs of calcareous water." Source: Wikipedia. Being aware that the nard was imported from India's Himalayan mountains to the Holy Lands, makes it easier to understand why the ointment was so costly. The woman proceeds to pour the ointment on Jesus' head. (John's account says Mary poured the ointment on Jesus' feet.)

Only John names Judas as the single villain condemning the woman's action. Mark and Matthew include all of the disciples present. John says the ointment was worth three hundred denarii. This would be equivalent to three years wages for a day laborer.

Angry reaction

**Mark 14:4-5;
Matthew 26:8-9;
John 12:4-6**

Angry reaction

**Mark 14:4-5;
Matthew 26:8-9;
John 12:4-6**

Mark 14:4-5
4 But there were some who said to themselves indignantly, "Why was the ointment thus wasted? 5 For this ointment might have been sold for more than three hundred denarii, and given to the poor." And they reproached her.

Matthew 26:8-9
8 But when the disciples saw it, they were indignant, saying, "Why this waste? 9 For this ointment might have been sold for a large sum, and given to the poor."

Comment
Some of the guests and all of the Inner-Circle were indignant at the obvious waste of the ointment. Some thought the ointment could have been sold for a hundred denarii. Others felt the amount could be as much as three hundred denarii. All agreed the expenditure should have gone to help the poor.

Only John names Judas as the single villain. Mark and Matthew include all of the disciples who were present.

John 12:4-6

4 But Judas Iscariot, one of his disciples (he who was to betray him), said, 5 "Why was this ointment not sold for three hundred denarii and given to the poor?" 6 This he said, not that he cared for the poor but because he was a thief, and as he had the money box he used to take what was put into it.

Jesus defends the woman

**Mark 14:6-9;
Matthew 26:10-13;
John 12:7-8**

Mark 14:6-9

6 But Jesus said, "Let her alone; why do you trouble her? She has done a beautiful thing to me. 7 For you always have the poor with you, and whenever you will, you can do good to them; but you will not always have me. 8 She has done what she could; she has anointed my body beforehand for burying. 9 And truly, I say to you, wherever the gospel is preached in the whole world, what she has done will be told in memory of her."

Matthew 26:10-13

10 But Jesus, aware of this, said to them, "Why do you trouble the woman? For she has done a beautiful thing to me. 11 For you

Jesus defends the woman

**Mark 14:6-9;
Matthew 26:10-13;
John 12:7-8**

Comment

Jesus defended the woman saying let her alone, why do you chastise her? He supported this with three separate strong proposals.

First, she had done a beautiful thing, preparing him for his burial.

Secondly, he spoke to the issue that had been raised as to why the ointment was not sold for a large sum of money. Jesus further said that the poor would be with them always. His continuing statement, cut them, and all mankind, like a knife through warm butter. You will always have the poor

always have the poor with you, but you will not always have me. [12] In pouring this ointment on my body she has done it to prepare me for burial. [13] Truly, I say to you, wherever this gospel is preached in the whole world, what she has done will be told in memory of her."

John 12:7-8
[7] Jesus said, "Let her alone, let her keep it for the day of my burial. [8] The poor you always have with you, but you do not always have me."

with you. Whenever you will, that is whenever you have the desire you can do for them. The opportunity is always there to help the poor, but it is a matter of what you choose to do or refuse to do that will make the difference.

Thirdly, he said what she has done will be remembered across the ages.

It is worth taking note that throughout Jesus' entire ministry he was constantly engaged in doing acts of goodness for people in need, the poor, sick, and destitute. Even so, he never made it a commandment that you must help the poor. He did not say, thou shall not, nor did he say, thou shall.

Judas stalks away

**Mark 14:10-11;
Matthew 26:14-16;
Luke 22:3-6**

Judas stalks away

**Mark 14:10-11;
Matthew 26:14-16;
Luke 22:3-6**

Mark 14:10-11
[10] Then Judas Iscariot, who was one of the twelve, went to the chief priests in order to betray him to them. [11] And when they heard it they were glad, and promised to give him money. And he sought an opportunity to betray him.

Comment
Mark, Matthew, and Luke agree it was Judas Iscariot who was the traitor. This was an act of treacherous villainy. The authorities were only too glad to welcome Judas into their midst. Like the women who anointed Jesus, but for absolutely

Matthew 26:14-16

14 Then one of the twelve, who was called Judas Iscariot, went to the chief priests 15 and said, "What will you give me if I deliver him to you?" And they paid him thirty pieces of silver. 16 And from that moment he sought an opportunity to betray him.

Luke 22:3-6

3 Then Satan entered into Judas called Iscariot, who was of the number of the twelve; 4 he went away and conferred with the chief priests and officers how he might betray him to them. 5 And they were glad, and engaged to give him money. 6 So he agreed, and sought an opportunity to betray him to them in the absence of the multitude.

different reasons, Judas' act would also be remembered throughout the ages.

Judas the traitor

There are a few researchers who point to the fact that the word betray has more than one meaning. In fact the word has been used in all of its five different definitions throughout the Bible.

The first of the five definitions defines betray as an act to give the betrayed into the hands of another person. The second usage of the word means to turn over a person to the power of another. It would be like a bounty hunter today who would go out and freelance to capture a wanted person. When the bounty hunter apprehends the fugitive and turns him over to the authorities he receives a reward.

Strong's Greek Dictionary Number 3860
Greek word: paradidomi [par-ad-id'-o-mee]
"didomi" means "to give"
Part of Speech: v
Usage Notes:
- deliver 53
- betray 40
- deliver up 10
- give 4
- give up 4
- give over 2
- commit 2
- misc 6 [Total Count: 121]

1. To give into the hands (of another)

2. To give over into (one's) power or use
   a) To deliver up one to custody, to be judged, condemned, punished, scourged, tormented, put to death
   b) To deliver up treacherously
   c) By betrayal to cause one to be taken
   d) To deliver one to be taught, molded

3. To commit, to commend

4. To deliver verbally
   a) Commands, rites
   b) To deliver by narrating, to report

5. To permit allow
   a) When the fruit will allow that is when its ripeness permits
   b) Gives itself up, presents itself

Was Judas selected by Jesus for the purpose of betraying him?

The case put forward by this group states that Judas was selected by Jesus for the purpose of betraying him. Their position further believes that Judas was the only member of the Inner-Circle who had the strength of character to exercise this distasteful mission. They believe all of the other eleven would not have been able to follow through and turn Jesus over to the authorities when the time came. Only Judas seems to fit the bill perfectly in their view.

Clarifying the term "Inner-Circle"

The word "Disciple" means student. Most moderns have narrowed the meaning to describe those twelve who traveled with Jesus throughout his ministry. A more careful reading of the Gospels reveals the use of the word disciple to include thousands of people who listened and learned from Jesus but did not give up their regular life to itinerate with him. It is obvious there was a distinction between the mass of disciples and the twelve disciples. To retain the distinction, I refer to the twelve as the "Inner-Circle."

Jesus' avowed mission was to revitalize Judaism, not to overthrow it and certainly not to overthrow the political government. In order for Jesus' mission to be accomplished he must have access to the chief priests to present his position. To give a modern example of this, it would be as if you wanted to the talk with the president of the United States. You could not just walk in the front door and be given an audience with the president. One who wishes to make an appointment with the president must go through a specific set of rules and channels in order to make his/her request. Ultimately your request would be granted or be rejected.

If Judas was successful in his attempt of betrayal in the sense of the turning Jesus over to the authorities it would mean that Jesus would have access to a face-to-face meeting with the chief priest. The successful act of betrayal would also necessitate the authorities to pay a reward to the betrayer who had facilitated the transaction.

Putting Judas' itinerary and activities during Holy Week into perspective

During the Passover meal in the upper-room, which would be Jesus' last meal with his Inner-Circle, Jesus announced that one of them would betray him. All of them ask, "Is it I Lord?" Finally, Peter, who was seated across from John at the triclinium mouthed the question, "Who is it?" Jesus also observed this silent communication and said to John, "It is the one who shares this sup with me." Then he dipped a piece of bread into the sauce or food dish and handed it to Judas. Judas then ate the morsel, as he was chewing Jesus told him to go and do quickly, what he must do.

Judas rose to his feet and left the room. None of the disciples had the slightest idea of where he was going. Upon arriving at the temple precincts, Judas was able to talk to someone, perhaps a representative of the chief priests, who had the authority to negotiate on behalf of the chief priest. When Judas revealed the purpose of this visit he was instantly greeted as an important person. For the chief priest this was an answer to his prayers. Negotiations followed as to how this betrayal would be handled, concluding with an agreement of the amount of money that was to be paid to Judas.

It was not until after the trial that Judas began to put together all of the pieces of what was taking place. The first thing that he learned was the Sanhedrin had found Jesus guilty of blasphemy. To make matters worse, they had ordered him to be put to death. Since they did not have the power under Roman authority to execute a person, they determined to go to Pilate and persuade him to issue the guilty verdict. Having never considered this turn of events a possibility Judas did not know what to do next. After much soul-searching, he attempted to return the blood money for the release of Jesus. To the authorities this was a ridiculous request that could not be taken seriously. Having failed in his attempt to redeem his action, Judas went out and hanged himself by the neck until dead.

A quick look at the Gospels' account

Judas is going to betray Jesus at some point in the future.

John 6:71; was to betray him.
John 12:4; disciples (he who was to betray him).

Judas did betray Jesus.

Matthew 10:4; who betrayed him.
Mark 3:19; who betrayed him.

Luke terms Judas a "traitor."

Luke 6:16; Judas Iscariot, who became a traitor.

This is the only mention of Judas as a "Traitor."

Matthew 26:25; "Is it I, Master?" He said to him, "You have said so."

> Could this be the place where Judas knew he was to be the "betrayer?"
> Was he looking for confirmation?
> Was he afraid of discovery?

John 13:26; "It is he to whom I shall give this morsel when I have dipped it." So when he had dipped the morsel, he gave it to Judas.

> Jesus reveals his knowledge of the pending betrayal.
> Was he thinking of Judas?
> Was this a "giving over in order to have a dialogue?"
> Was it to be a "handing over for trial and conviction?"

Judas goes to the Chief Priest.

Mark 14:10; went to the chief priests in order to betray him to them.
Matthew 26:14; Judas Iscariot, went to the chief priests.

> How would Judas achieve seeing the high priest?
> Did he have to work his way up the chain of command?

Whatever Judas may have had in mind when Satan took control; Satan's plan took dominance.

Luke 22:3; Then Satan entered into Judas called Iscariot,

John 13:2; during supper, when the devil had already put it into the heart of Judas Iscariot, Simon's son, to betray him,

John 13:28-29; Then after the morsel, Satan entered into him. Jesus said to him, "What you are going to do, do quickly." Now no one at the table knew why he said this to him. Some thought that, because Judas had the money box,

> Satan used Judas; he was not going to let him dictate what was to be done!

As promised by Satan he was "seeing" Jesus at a more opportune time.

Judas knew Jesus had regularly returned to the Garden of Gethsemane each evening after leaving Jerusalem.

John 18: 2-3-5; Now Judas, who betrayed him, also knew the place; for Jesus often met there with his disciples.

Judas needed the assurance of an armed band to accomplish his mission.

Luke 2:47; Judas, one of the twelve, was leading them

John 18:3; So Judas, procuring a band of soldiers and some officers from the chief priests and the Pharisees, went there with lanterns and torches and weapons.

Mark 14:43; with him a crowd with swords and clubs, from the chief priests and the scribes and the elders.

Matthew 26:47; with him a great crowd with swords and clubs, from the chief priests and the elders

It seems Jesus was not aware of any plan for Judas to betray him.

John 18:4; Then Jesus, knowing all that was to befall him, came forward and said to them, "Whom do you seek?"

If Jesus had bought into Judas' plan why would he ask why they had come armed to arrest him?

John 18:5; They answered him, "Jesus of Nazareth." Jesus said to them, "I am he." Judas, who betrayed him, was standing with them.

The kiss was the ultimate insult!

Luke 22:48; Jesus said to him, "Judas, would you betray the Son of man with a kiss?"

His repentance was unexpected. Only found in Matthew.

Matthew 27:3; saw that he was condemned, he repented and brought
          back the thirty pieces of silver to the chief priests and
          the elders,

Judas had never considered Jesus' death as a possibility. The Sanhedrin
did not have the power to execute. Judas never though Pilate would
become involved.

Plotting to kill Jesus and Lazarus

Luke 22:1-2;
Mark 14:1b-2;
Matthew 26:3-5;
John 12:11

Luke 22:1-2
1 Now the feast of Unleavened Bread drew near, which is called the Passover. 2 And the chief priests and the scribes were seeking how to put him to death; for they feared the people.

Mark 14:1b-2
1 And the chief priests and the scribes were seeking how to arrest him by stealth, and kill him; 2 for they said, "Not during the feast, less there be a tumult of the people."

Matthew 26:3-5
3 Then the chief priests and the elders of the people gathered in the palace of the high priest, who was called Ca'iaphas, 4 and took counsel together in order

---

Plotting to kill Jesus and Lazarus

Luke 22:1-2;
Mark 14:1b-2;
Matthew 26:3-5;
John 12:11

Comment
All four Evangelists agree that a plot tó kill Jesus was decided upon. They also agreed the plot must be sprung after the feast not during the celebration. Matthew said this meeting took place at the palace of Caiaphas, the High Priest. John alone stated that they also intended to kill Lazarus.

to arrest Jesus by stealth and kill him. 5 But they said, "Not during the feast, lest there be a tumult among the people."

John 12:11
because on account of him many of the Jews were going away and believing in Jesus.

The meals at Bethany

The meals at Bethany serve as our prelude to the beginning of Holy Week. The reports of Mark and Matthew differ from John on several points.

First is the matter of location. Mark and Matthew said their meal took place with Simon the Leper. John said his meal was at the home of Lazarus and his two sisters.

Secondly, the mention of how many days it was until Passover. Mark and Matthew said Passover was two days away. John said Passover was six days away.

Third, who poured the ointment? Mark and Matthew leave the woman unidentified. John tells us it was Mary.

Fourth, upon what part of the body was the ointment poured? Mark and Matthew said it was poured on Jesus' head. John said it was poured on his feet.

In my opinion we definitely have two different events that have several similarities.

Chapter 2

Holy Week: Monday

Jesus enters Jerusalem	*Jesus enters Jerusalem*
Bring the colt	*Bring the colt*
Mark 11:1-7; **Matthew 21:1-7;** **Luke 19:28-35**	**Mark 11:1-7;** **Matthew 21:1-7;** **Luke 19:28-35**

Mark 11:1-7

1 And when they drew near to Jerusalem, to Beth'phage and Bethany, at the Mount of Olives, he sent two of his disciples, 2 and said to them, "Go into the village opposite you, and immediately as you enter it you will find a colt tied, on which no one has ever sat; untie it and bring it. 3 If any one says to you, 'Why are you doing this?' say, 'The Lord has need of it and will send it back here immediately.'" 4 And they went away, and found a colt tied at the door out in the open street; and they untied it. 5 And those who stood there said to them, "What are you doing, untying the colt?" 6 And they told them what Jesus had said; and they let them go. 7 And they brought the colt to Jesus, and threw their garments on it; and he sat upon it.

Comment

Jesus, with the Inner-Circle left Bethany and headed toward Jerusalem. As they neared the crest of the Mount of Olives they came to the village known as Bethphage. At this point, Jesus sent two of his, unnamed, disciples into the village to locate a colt and bring it to him.

Obviously Jesus knew the owner would oblige them when he was told why the animal was needed. The owner did ask why they were taking the colt and permitted it when they explained, the Master needed it.

Matthew said the request was to fulfill the words of the prophet Zechariah.

Matthew 21:1-7
1 And when they drew near to Jerusalem and came to Beth'phage, to the Mount of Olives, then Jesus sent two disciples, 2 saying to them, "Go into the village opposite you, and immediately you will find an ass tied, and a colt with her; untie them and bring them to me. 3 If any one says anything to you, you shall say, 'The Lord has need of them,' and he will send them immediately." 4 This took place to fulfil what was spoken by the prophet, saying,
5 "Tell the daughter of Zion,
Behold, your king is coming to you,
humble, and mounted on an ass,
and on a colt, the foal of an ass."
6 The disciples went and did as Jesus had directed them; 7 they brought the ass and the colt, and put their garments on them, and he sat thereon.

Luke 19:28-35
28 And when he had said this, he went on ahead, going up to Jerusalem. 29 When he drew near to Beth'phage and Bethany, at the mount that is called Olivet, he sent two of the disciples, 30 saying, "Go into the village opposite, where on entering you will find a colt tied, on which no one has ever yet sat; untie it and bring it here. 31 If any one asks you, 'Why are you

Rejoice greatly, O daughter of Zion! Shout aloud, O daughter of Jerusalem! Lo, your king comes to you; triumphant and victorious is he, humble and riding on an ass, on a colt the foal of an ass. – Zechariah 9:9

Mark tells us the colt had never been ridden. Matthew tells us that they brought both the ass and the colt. This would be logical, because the ass would have had a calming effect upon the colt.

untying it?' you shall say this, 'The Lord has need of it.'" 32 So those who were sent went away and found it as he had told them. 33 And as they were untying the colt, its owners said to them, "Why are you untying the colt?" 34 And they said, "The Lord has need of it." 35 And they brought it to Jesus, and throwing their garments on the colt they set Jesus upon it.

Our Palm Sunday observance

**Mark 11:8-10;
Matthew 21:8-11;
Luke 19:36-40;
John 12:12-19**

Mark 11:8-10
8 And many spread their garments on the road, and others spread leafy branches which they had cut from the fields. 9 And those who went before and those who followed cried out, "Hosanna! Blessed is he who comes in the name of the Lord! 10 Blessed is the kingdom of our father David that is coming! Hosanna in the highest!"

Matthew 21:8-11
8 Most of the crowd spread their garments on the road, and others cut branches from the trees and spread them on the road. 9 And the crowds that went before him and that followed him shouted, "Hosanna to the Son of David!

Our Palm Sunday observance

**Mark 11:8-10;
Matthew 21:8-11;
Luke 19:36-40;
John 12:12-19**

Comment

As Jesus descended the Mount of Olives, riding on the back of the colt, many began to pay him homage. Some laid their garments on the path, while others cut branches and laid them along the path that the colt might walk on them. They began to shout, "Hosanna to the son of David. Blessed is he who comes in the name of the Lord." The Hebrew word hosanna means, "To save." Some asked, "Who is this?" Among the responses was "This is Jesus of Nazareth, the prophet."

Those who cut palm branches lifted them into the air and waved them shouting, "Hosanna,

Blessed is he who comes in the name of the Lord! Hosanna in the highest!" 10 And when he entered Jerusalem, all the city was stirred, saying, "Who is this?" 11 And the crowds said, "This is the prophet Jesus from Nazareth of Galilee."

Luke 19:36-40

36 And as he rode along, they spread their garments on the road. 37 As he was now drawing near, at the descent of the Mount of Olives, the whole multitude of the disciples began to rejoice and praise God with a loud voice for all the mighty works that they had seen, 38 saying, "Blessed is the King who comes in the name of the Lord! Peace in heaven and glory in the highest!" 39 And some of the Pharisees in the multitude said to him, "Teacher, rebuke your disciples." 40 He answered, "I tell you, if these were silent, the very stones would cry out."

John 12:12-19

12 The next day a great crowd who had come to the feast heard that Jesus was coming to Jerusalem. 13 So they took branches of palm trees and went out to meet him, crying, "Hosanna! Blessed is he who comes in the name of the Lord, even the King of Israel!" 14 And Jesus found a young ass and sat upon it; as it is written,

the Savior is coming!" Whether intentionally or unintentionally, were using a symbol of the Zealot movement. Waving the palm branch was a call to arms signal announcing, "Now is time to strike, it is time to fight, we go to war, our King leads us!"

The Fortress of Antonia was attached to the Temple Mount on the northern side. The troops Pilate brought from Caesarea were stationed there during the Passover.

As Jesus came near to the gates of Jerusalem the shouts could be heard far and wide, "Hosanna in the highest," meaning God is coming! The Messiah is here! The sentries along the wall undoubtedly had a reflex action to the scene before them. Hearing the shouts of "hosanna" and seeing the throng of people moving toward the Temple placed them on high alert for potential trouble.

The soldiers were looking at a contradiction. Coming toward the city gate was a shouting, cheering mob waving the palms branches in the sense of a military revolt. The leader however was riding on a humble donkey. Confused and bewildered and yet ready for anything stood the garrison and their commander.

15 "Fear not, daughter of Zion; behold, your king is coming, sitting on an ass' colt!"
16 His disciples did not understand this at first; but when Jesus was glorified, then they remembered that this had been written of him and had been done to him. 17 The crowd that had been with him when he called Laz'arus out of the tomb and raised him from the dead bore witness. 18 The reason why the crowd went to meet him was that they heard he had done this sign. 19 The Pharisees then said to one another, "You see that you can do nothing; look, the world has gone after him."

Jesus symbolized to all who had eyes to see that he had not come as a conquering warrior but as the solitary servant of God.

Jesus wept over Jerusalem

Luke 19:41-44
41 And when he drew near and saw the city he wept over it, 42 saying, "Would that even today you knew the things that make for peace! But now they are hid from your eyes. 43 For the days shall come upon you, when your enemies will cast up a bank about you and surround you, and hem you in on every side, 44 and dash you to the ground, you and your children within you, and they will not leave one stone upon another in you; because you did not know the time of your visitation."

Jesus wept over Jerusalem

Luke 19:41-44

Comment
This is an independent statement found only in Luke.

It is significant that this is the second time the Gospels tell of Jesus weeping. He wept first over Lazarus, his friend, and now he wept over the future of the city and the people of Jerusalem.

Jesus enters Jerusalem *Differing accounts*	*Jesus enters Jerusalem* *Differing accounts*
Mark 11:11 And he entered Jerusalem, and went into the temple; and when he had looked round at everything, as it was already late, he went out to Bethany with the twelve.	**Mark 11:11** **Comment** Mark tells us Jesus entered Jerusalem and went directly to the temple. He looked around and because it was already late in the afternoon he left and returned to Bethany, with his Inner-Circle. Matthew and Luke give a slightly different version and we will examine them in chapter 3.

Chapter 3

Holy Week: Tuesday

The Fig tree	*The Fig Tree*
Mark 11:12-14; **Matthew 21:18-22**	**Mark 11:12-14;** **Matthew 21:18-22**

Mark 11:12-14

12 On the following day, when they came from Bethany, he was hungry. 13 And seeing in the distance a fig tree in leaf, he went to see if he could find anything on it. When he came to it, he found nothing but leaves, for it was not the season for figs. 14 And he said to it, "May no one ever eat fruit from you again." And his disciples heard it.

Matthew 21:18-22

18 In the morning, as he was returning to the city, he was hungry. 19 And seeing a fig tree by the wayside he went to it, and found nothing on it but leaves only. And he said to it, "May no fruit ever come from you again!" And the fig tree withered at once. 20 When the disciples saw it they marveled, saying, "How did the fig tree wither at once?" 21 And Jesus answered them, "Truly, I say to you, if you have faith and never doubt, you will

Comment

Tuesday morning, as Jesus made his way from Bethany to Jerusalem he was hungry. He came upon a fig tree covered with leaves. This was strange because it was not the season for figs. And sure enough, he found no fruit upon the tree. Jesus spoke to the tree saying, "May no one ever eat fruit from you again." Hearing these words, the disciples may have been quite astounded.

Under normal circumstances, the fig tree never puts out leaves until the fruit is ready.

not only do what has been done to the fig tree, but even if you say to this mountain, 'Be taken up and cast into the sea,' it will be done. 22 And whatever you ask in prayer, you will receive, if you have faith."

Luke has a similar story

Luke 13:6-9
6 And he told this parable: "A man had a fig tree planted in his vineyard; and he came seeking fruit on it and found none. 7 And he said to the vinedresser, 'Lo, these three years I have come seeking fruit on this fig tree, and I find none. Cut it down; why should it use up the ground?' 8 And he answered him, 'Let it alone, sir, this year also, till I dig about it and put on manure. 9 And if it bears fruit next year, well and good; but if not, you can cut it down.'"

Luke has a similar story

Luke 13:6-9

Comment
The setting is quite different. There is a dialogue between the vinedresser and the owner of the vineyard. The vinedresser pleads for the life of the tree promising to tend it and see if it would produce in the next season. The implication of this story was to give nonbelievers a little longer before judging them.

Cleansing the Temple

Mark 11:15-19;
Matthew 21:12-13;
Luke 19:45-46

Mark 11:15-19
15 And they came to Jerusalem. And he entered the temple and began to drive out those who sold and those who bought in

Cleansing the Temple

Mark 11:15-19;
Matthew 21:12-13;
Luke 19:45-46

Comment
Without doubt, there are differences in the statements of the four evangelists concerning the cleansing of the temple.

the temple, and he overturned the tables of the money-changers and the seats of those who sold pigeons; 16 and he would not allow any one to carry anything through the temple. 17 And he taught, and said to them, "Is it not written, 'My house shall be called a house of prayer for all the nations'? But you have made it a den of robbers." 18 And the chief priests and the scribes heard it and sought a way to destroy him; for they feared him, because all the multitude was astonished at his teaching. 19 And when evening came they went out of the city.

Matthew 21:12-13

12 And Jesus entered the temple of God and drove out all who sold and bought in the temple, and he overturned the tables of the money-changers and the seats of those who sold pigeons. 13 He said to them, "It is written, 'My house shall be called a house of prayer'; but you make it a den of robbers."

Luke 19:45-46

45 And he entered the temple and began to drive out those who sold, 46 saying to them, "It is written, 'My house shall be a house of prayer'; but you have made it a den of robbers."

John said the first cleansing by Jesus was on his first visit to the Temple, following his baptism. Mark, Matthew, and Luke state the cleansing took place on Tuesday of Holy Week. We may make note of two differences between these reports. First, there is a significant difference between John's report and that of the other three evangelists. Second, the reports of Mark, Matthew, and Luke are almost identical except for the time of the occurrence.

The significance of this event is borne out in the fact that all four evangelists report such an occurrence as having taken place.

Is this the second telling of the same story?

Some interpreters believe this is a retelling of the event in John of Jesus' first cleansing of the temple. I feel these are two separate and specific incidents. In John's version, Jesus made a whip of cords and drove out the moneychangers and others. John said this happened on the first trip Jesus made to Jerusalem following his baptism. In this instance Mark, Matthew, and Luke say it was in Holy Week that Jesus cleansed the temple.

Greeks are among the Pilgrims	*Greeks are among the Pilgrims*
John 12:20-26 20 Now among those who went up to worship at the feast were some Greeks. 21 So these came to Philip, who was from Beth-sa'ida in Galilee, and said to him, "Sir, we wish to see Jesus." 22 Philip went and told Andrew; Andrew went with Philip and they told Jesus. 23 And Jesus answered them, "The hour has come for the Son of man to be glorified. 24 Truly, truly, I say to you, unless a grain of wheat falls into the earth and dies, it remains alone; but if it dies, it bears much fruit. 25 He who loves his life loses it, and he who hates his life in this world will keep it for eternal life. 26 If any one serves me, he must follow me; and where I am, there shall my servant be also; if any one serves me, the Father will honor him.	**John 12:20-26** **Comment** This is a confusing passage. There were some Greeks present at the Passover feast. They asked Philip if they could meet with Jesus. Philip obviously could not provide the answer so he went to confer with Andrew. Both Philip and Andrew went to Jesus, but Jesus did not answer, instead he delivered a discourse on what the future holds. Referring to himself as the Son of man, he proclaimed he would be glorified in his death. He told a short parable of the kernel of wheat being put into the ground so that it apparently dies. When it germinates it puts forth the shoot that brings the ears that bring many kernels thereby multiplying and being fruitful. Then Jesus repeated his earlier statements of losing life to find life.

For this purpose I have come to this hour

John 12:27-36a

27 "Now is my soul troubled. And what shall I say? 'Father, save me from this hour'? No, for this purpose I have come to this hour. 28 Father, glorify thy name." Then a voice came from heaven, "I have glorified it, and I will glorify it again." 29 The crowd standing by heard it and said that it had thundered. Others said, "An angel has spoken to him." 30 Jesus answered, "This voice has come for your sake, not for mine. 31 Now is the judgment of this world, now shall the ruler of this world be cast out; 32 and I, when I am lifted up from the earth, will draw all men to myself." 33 He said this to show by what death he was to die. 34 The crowd answered him, "We have heard from the law that the Christ remains forever. How can you say that the Son of man must be lifted up? Who is this Son of man?" 35 Jesus said to them, "The light is with you for a little longer. Walk while you have the light, lest the darkness overtake you; he who walks in the darkness does not know where he goes. 36 While you have the light, believe in the light, that you may become sons of light."

For this purpose I have come to this hour

John 12:27-36a

Comment

Even though Jesus was very troubled over the pending future he would not ask his Father to save him from it, because this was why he came to dwell among men on earth. Jesus' death would glorify both he and the Father.

Without warning God spoke from heaven. The crowd heard what they thought was thunder. Some said it was an angel speaking to Jesus. Jesus breaks in telling them this voice was for their benefit not his.

Jesus said to them now is the judgment on the world and the ruler of this world will be cast out. Jesus next told them how he would die. He would be lifted up as part of the crucifixion experience. The crowd paid no attention to the statement. They were too interested in asking Jesus to explain something to them. "We have heard the Christ will live forever, is that true? Who is the son of man," they asked. Jesus' answer was the contrast of light and darkness. Virtually everyone hearing this reply understood it to be a comment, common to the Essenes (sons of light / sons of darkness).

Many of the authorities believed in Him

John 12:36b-43

36 When Jesus had said this, he departed and hid himself from them.37 Though he had done so many signs before them, yet they did not believe in him; 38 it was that the word spoken by the prophet Isaiah might be fulfilled: "Lord, who has believed our report, and to whom has the arm of the Lord been revealed?" 39 Therefore they could not believe. For Isaiah again said, 40 "He has blinded their eyes and hardened their heart, lest they should see with their eyes and perceive with their heart, and turn for me to heal them." 41 Isaiah said this because he saw his glory and spoke of him. 42 Nevertheless many even of the authorities believed in him, but for fear of the Pharisees they did not confess it, lest they should be put out of the synagogue: 43 for they loved the praise of men more than the praise of God.

I have come as light into the world

John 12:44-50

44 And Jesus cried out and said, "He who believes in me, believes not in me but in him who sent me. 45 And he who sees me

Many of the authorities believed in Him

John 12:36b-43

Comment

After Jesus departed from this group he avoided them wherever possible. They had witnessed many of his signs, (miracles) yet they still did not believe. John explained this as being part of God's will, citing Isaiah the prophet.

Who has believed what we have heard? And to whom has the arm of the LORD been revealed? – Isaiah 53:1

Even though most rejected Jesus some of the authorities did believe in him. However, they would not confess this openly fearing they would be cast out of the synagogue. John accuses them of loving the praise of men more than the praise of God.

I have come as light into the world

John 12:44-50
Comment

Jesus tried to explain his relationship to God. To believe in him also meant believing in

sees him who sent me. [46] I have come as light into the world, that whoever believes in me may not remain in darkness. [47] If any one hears my sayings and does not keep them, I do not judge him; for I did not come to judge the world but to save the world. [48] He who rejects me and does not receive my sayings has a judge; the word that I have spoken will be his judge on the last day. [49] For I have not spoken on my own authority; the Father who sent me has himself given me commandment what to say and what to speak. [50] And I know that his commandment is eternal life. What I say, therefore, I say as the Father has bidden me."

God who had sent him. When Jesus said, "I am the light of the world," many in the audience would interpret him as claiming to be the fulfillment of Essene theology. A staple of the Essene theology was they were sons of light, and everyone else were sons of darkness.

Jesus said he did not come to judge them but to save the world. However, anyone who rejected him or his sayings had a judge waiting at the last day. Jesus said he did not teach of his own authority but at the pleasure of God.

Healed those who came to him

Matthew 21:14-17
[14] And the blind and the lame came to him in the temple, and he healed them. [15] But when the chief priests and the scribes saw the wonderful things that he did, and the children crying out in the temple, "Hosanna to the Son of David!" they were indignant; [16] and they said to him, "Do you hear what these are saying?" And Jesus said to them, "Yes; have you never read, 'Out of the mouth of babes and sucklings thou hast brought perfect praise'?"

Healed those who came to him

Matthew 21:14-17

Comment
As it had been in all the territory outside Jerusalem, the sick and lame were brought to him for healing. Every positive response of the people toward Jesus made the Pharisees more indignant than before. The Pharisees angrily asked Jesus if he was deaf to what the people were saying. Jesus answered with a quote from the Psalms.

17 And leaving them, he went out of the city to Bethany and lodged there.

Out of the mouth of babes and sucklings hast thou ordained strength because of thine enemies, that thou mightiest still the enemy and the avenger. – Psalms 8:2 (KJV)

Challenge to Jesus' authority

**Mark 11:27-33;
Matthew 21:23-27;
Luke 20:1-8**

Mark 11:27-33
27 And they came again to Jerusalem. And as he was walking in the temple, the chief priests and the scribes and the elders came to him, 28 and they said to him, "By what authority are you doing these things, or who gave you this authority to do them?" 29 Jesus said to them, "I will ask you a question; answer me, and I will tell you by what authority I do these things. 30 Was the baptism of John from heaven or from men? Answer me." 31 And they argued with one another, "If we say, 'From heaven,' he will say, 'Why then did you not believe him?' 32 But shall we say, 'From men'?' -- they were afraid of the people, for all held that John was a real prophet. 33 So they answered Jesus, "We do not know." And Jesus said to them, "Neither will I tell you by what authority I do these things."

Challenge to Jesus' authority

**Mark 11:27-33;
Matthew 21:23-27;
Luke 20:1-8**

Comment
These three accounts are basically the same. This still leaves the ambiguity concerning Mark's dating of Monday and Matthew referring to Tuesday. Luke is neutral in that he makes no mention relative to a particular day. John does not mention the question of authority.

The day following the cleansing, the chief priest and scribes find Jesus walking through the temple. They confront him with the question, "By what authority do you do these things?" At this point the "things" would be healing, teaching, and cleansing the Temple.

Jesus offered to answer their question if they would first answer one for him. This question was, "Was the baptism of John from heaven or from men?" The chief priests and the scribes put their heads together

Matthew 21:23-27

23 And when he entered the temple, the chief priests and the elders of the people came up to him as he was teaching, and said, "By what authority are you doing these things, and who gave you this authority?" 24 Jesus answered them, "I also will ask you a question; and if you tell me the answer, then I also will tell you by what authority I do these things. 25 The baptism of John, whence was it? From heaven or from men?" And they argued with one another, "If we say, 'From heaven,' he will say to us, 'Why then did you not believe him?' 26 But if we say, 'From men,' we are afraid of the multitude; for all hold that John was a prophet." 27 So they answered Jesus, "We do not know." And he said to them, "Neither will I tell you by what authority I do these things.

Luke 20:1-8

1 One day, as he was teaching the people in the temple and preaching the gospel, the chief priests and the scribes with the elders came up 2 and said to him, "Tell us by what authority you do these things, or who it is that gave you this authority." 3 He answered them, "I also will ask you a question; now tell me, 4 Was the baptism of John from heaven or from men?" 5 And they discussed it with one another, and deliberated Jesus' question. Finding no suitable answer they chose to say, "We do not know." Jesus replied, "Then I am not going to give you an answer either."

saying, "If we say, 'From heaven,' he will say, 'Why did you not believe him?' 6 But if we say, 'From men,' all the people will stone us; for they are convinced that John was a prophet.' 7 So they answered that they did not know whence it was. 8 And Jesus said to them, "Neither will I tell you by what authority I do these things."

Parable of two sons

Matthew 21:28-32
28 "What do you think? A man had two sons; and he went to the first and said, 'Son, go and work in the vineyard today.' 29 And he answered, 'I will not'; but afterward he repented and went. 30 And he went to the second and said the same; and he answered, 'I go, sir,' but did not go. 31 Which of the two did the will of his father?" They said, "The first." Jesus said to them, "Truly, I say to you, the tax collectors and the harlots go into the kingdom of God before you. 32 For John came to you in the way of righteousness, and you did not believe him, but the tax collectors and the harlots believed him; and even when you saw it, you did not afterward repent and believe him.

Parable of two sons

Matthew 21:28-32

Comment
Jesus then spoke this parable to the chief priests and scribes. There was a man with two sons, he told the first to go and work in the vineyard for a day. The son said no, but then went and worked in the vineyard. Later he told the second son to go and work in the vineyard, the son said yes but he never went.

Which of the two sons did the father's bidding asked Jesus? They answered the first one. With a sternness that would stun the hardiest of listeners Jesus said, "John came to you with righteousness, and you would not believe him. Do not be surprised that tax collectors, harlots, and sinners will enter the kingdom of God before you."

Absent Landlord

Mark 12:1-9;
Matthew 21:33-41;
Luke 20:9-16

Mark 12:1-9

[1] And he began to speak to them in parables. "A man planted a vineyard, and set a hedge around it, and dug a pit for the wine press, and built a tower, and let it out to tenants, and went into another country. [2] When the time came, he sent a servant to the tenants, to get from them some of the fruit of the vineyard. [3] And they took him and beat him, and sent him away empty-handed. [4] Again he sent to them another servant, and they wounded him in the head, and treated him shamefully. [5] And he sent another, and him they killed; and so with many others, some they beat and some they killed. [6] He had still one other, a beloved son; finally he sent him to them, saying, 'They will respect my son.' [7] But those tenants said to one another, 'This is the heir; come, let us kill him, and the inheritance will be ours.' [8] And they took him and killed him, and cast him out of the vineyard. [9] What will the owner of the vineyard do? He will come and destroy the tenants, and give the vineyard to others.

Absent Landlord

Mark 12:1-9;
Matthew 21:33-41;
Luke 20:9-16

Comment

Jesus continued to speak in parables. The content of this story was very familiar to most of his listeners. The man planted a vineyard, then he planted hedges to mark its boundaries, next he built a tower for guarding it, and when all was ready he rented it to tenants.

With his business concluded he took his leave to go to a distant country. At harvest time, he sent servants to collect his portion. Unbelievably the tenants beat the servants and sent them away empty handed. The man sent another servant and they treated him badly, wounding him in the head. The next servant he sent they killed. As a last resort he sent his beloved son believing they would respect him. When the tenants saw that it was the son they plotted to kill him and take the inheritance. And so they killed him and threw his body out of the vineyard.

Then Jesus asked, "What do you think the owner will do?" Without hesitation, the chief priests and scribes said the owner would come and destroy the tenants and give the vineyard to others.

Matthew 21:33-41

33 "Hear another parable. There was a householder who planted a vineyard, and set a hedge around it, and dug a wine press in it, and built a tower, and let it out to tenants, and went into another country. 34 When the season of fruit drew near, he sent his servants to the tenants, to get his fruit; 35 and the tenants took his servants and beat one, killed another, and stoned another. 36 Again he sent other servants, more than the first; and they did the same to them. 37 Afterward he sent his son to them, saying, 'They will respect my son.' 38 But when the tenants saw the son, they said to themselves, 'This is the heir; come, let us kill him and have his inheritance.' 39 And they took him and cast him out of the vineyard, and killed him. 40 When therefore the owner of the vineyard comes, what will he do to those tenants?" 41 They said to him, "He will put those wretches to a miserable death, and let out the vineyard to other tenants who will give him the fruits in their seasons."

Luke 20:9-16

9 And he began to tell the people this parable: "A man planted a vineyard, and let it out to tenants, and went into another country for a long while. 10 When the time came, he sent a servant to

the tenants, that they should give him some of the fruit of the vineyard; but the tenants beat him, and sent him away empty-handed. [11] And he sent another servant; him also they beat and treated shamefully, and sent him away empty-handed. [12] And he sent yet a third; this one they wounded and cast out. [13] Then the owner of the vineyard said, 'What shall I do? I will send my beloved son; it may be they will respect him.' [14] But when the tenants saw him, they said to themselves, 'This is the heir; let us kill him, that the inheritance may be ours.' [15] And they cast him out of the vineyard and killed him. What then will the owner of the vineyard do to them? [16] He will come and destroy those tenants, and give the vineyard to others." When they heard this, they said, "God forbid!'"

Stone rejected by the builder

**Mark 12:10-11;
Matthew 21:42-43;
Luke 20:17-18**

Mark 12:10-11

[10] Have you not read this scripture: 'The very stone which the builders rejected has become the head of the corner; [11] this was the Lord's doing, and it is marvelous in our eyes'?"

Stone rejected by the builder

**Mark 12:10-11;
Matthew 21:42-43;
Luke 20:17-18**

Comment

Jesus then told them a parable of the stone and its rejection. Others came and took the stone and made it the head of the corner. This was the most important stone in any building. It had to be flawless; perfect in every way.

Matthew 21:42-43

42 Jesus said to them, "Have you never read in the scriptures: 'The very stone which the builders rejected has become the head of the corner; this was the Lord's doing, and it is marvelous in our eyes'?
43 Therefore I tell you, the kingdom of God will be taken away from you and given to a nation producing the fruits of it."

Luke 20:17-18

17 But he looked at them and said, "What then is this that is written: 'The very stone which the builders rejected has become the head of the corner'? 18 Every one who falls on that stone will be broken to pieces; but when it falls on any one it will crush him."

They understood at once Jesus was quoting the psalms to them:

22 *The stone which the builders refused is become the head stone of the corner.* 23 *This is the LORD'S doing; it is marvelous in our eyes.* – Psalms 118:22-23

__Angry Response__

**Mark 12:12;
Matthew 21:45-46**

__Angry Response__

**Mark 12:12;
Matthew 21:45-46**

Mark 12:12

And they tried to arrest him, but feared the multitude, for they perceived that he had told the parable against them; so they left him and went away.

Comment

The authorities were so enraged they would have arrested him on the spot had they not feared the crowd.

Matthew 21:45-46
45 When the chief priests and the Pharisees heard his parables, they perceived that he was speaking about them. 46 But when they tried to arrest him, they feared the multitudes, because they held him to be a prophet.

Teaching daily

Luke 19:47-48
47 And he was teaching daily in the temple. The chief priests and the scribes and the principal men of the people sought to destroy him; 48 but they did not find anything they could do, for all the people hung upon his words.

Back to Mount of Olives

Luke 21:37-38
37 And every day he was teaching in the temple, but at night he went out and lodged on the mount called Olivet. 38 And early in the morning all the people came to him in the temple to hear him.

Teaching daily

Luke 19:47-48

Comment
Luke makes a general statement that Jesus was in the temple teaching each day.

Back to Mount of Olives

Luke 21:37-38

Comment
Sunday, Monday, and Tuesday nights of Holy Week, Jesus lodged outside the city of Jerusalem. He did this because he knew of the plots to kill him. He also knew his time had not yet come. The time would come on Wednesday evening.

Chapter 4

Holy Week: Wednesday Morning

Essene's Passover

First day of Unleavened Bread

**Mark 14:12-16;
Matthew 26:17-19;
Luke 22:7-13**

Mark 14:12-16

12 And on the first day of Unleavened Bread, when they sacrificed the passover lamb, his disciples said to him, "Where will you have us go and prepare for you to eat the passover?" 13 And he sent two of his disciples, and said to them, "Go into the city, and a man carrying a jar of water will meet you; follow him, 14 and wherever he enters, say to the householder, 'The Teacher says, Where is my guest room, where I am to eat the passover with my disciples?' 15 And he will show you a large upper room furnished and ready; there prepare for us." 16 And the disciples set out and went to the city, and found it as he had told them; and they prepared the passover.

Essene's Passover

First day of Unleavened Bread

**Mark 14:12-16;
Matthew 26:17-19;
Luke 22:7-13**

Comment

Mark reports the basic story with Matthew and Luke making small additions.

The Inner-Circle did not realize this would be Jesus' last Passover celebration with them.

They raised the question of where he would like the Passover meal prepared. Jesus told them to go into Jerusalem, and they would meet a man carrying a jar of water, and they were to follow him.

It has always been interpreted that a man carrying a jar of water would have been a profoundly unusual sight. However, we have learned that in the Essene community, a celibate man would have every reason to carry his own water.

Matthew 26:17-19
17 Now on the first day of Unleavened Bread the disciples came to Jesus, saying, "Where will you have us prepare for you to eat the passover?" 18 He said, "Go into the city to a certain one, and say to him, 'The Teacher says, My time is at hand; I will keep the passover at your house with my disciples.'" 19 And the disciples did as Jesus had directed them, and they prepared the passover.

Luke 22:7-13
7 Then came the day of Unleavened Bread, on which the passover lamb had to be sacrificed. 8 So Jesus sent Peter and John, saying, "Go and prepare the passover for us, that we may eat it." 9 They said to him, "Where will you have us prepare it?" 10 He said to them, "Behold, when you have entered the city, a man carrying a jar of water will meet you; follow him into the house which he enters, 11 and tell the householder, 'The Teacher says to you, Where is the guest room, where I am to eat the passover with my disciples?' 12 And he will show you a large upper room furnished; there make ready." 13 And they went, and found it as he had told them; and they prepared the passover.

The disciples were instructed to follow this man where ever he went. The householder would show them the room that had been prepared for the feast.

Matthew adds Jesus saying, "My time is at hand."

The Fig tree has withered

Mark 11:20-25

20 As they passed by in the morning, they saw the fig tree withered away to its roots. 21 And Peter remembered and said to him, "Master, look! The fig tree which you cursed has withered." 22 And Jesus answered them, "Have faith in God. 23 Truly, I say to you, whoever says to this mountain, 'Be taken up and cast into the sea,' and does not doubt in his heart, but believes that what he says will come to pass, it will be done for him. 24 Therefore I tell you, whatever you ask in prayer, believe that you have received it, and it will be yours. 25 And whenever you stand praying, forgive, if you have anything against any one; so that your Father also who is in heaven may forgive you your trespasses."

Resumes teaching in the Temple

Matthew 22:1-14

1 And again Jesus spoke to them in parables, saying, 2 "The kingdom of heaven may be compared to a king who gave a marriage feast for his son, 3 and sent his servants to call those who were invited to the marriage feast; but they would not come. 4 Again he sent

The Fig tree has withered

Mark 11:20-25

Comment

Mark tells us the story of the fig tree that Jesus cursed and its withering in two separate passages, (Mark 11:12-14 and 11:20-25). Matthew rolls it all into one event.

The major point of this story centers upon Jesus telling them to have faith in God. This kind of faith means there is no doubt that God will do what you ask. The second major point of the story is we must forgive others their trespasses against us so that God will forgive us. This is the same admonition we find in what we call the Lord's Prayer.

Resumes teaching in the Temple

Matthew 22:1-14

Comment

Jesus told the story of a king wanting to have a great feast in honor of his son's upcoming wedding. He sent invitations to all of the nobility and upper crust. When the day of the feast

other servants, saying, 'Tell those who are invited, Behold, I have made ready my dinner, my oxen and my fat calves are killed, and everything is ready; come to the marriage feast.' 5 But they made light of it and went off, one to his farm, another to his business, 6 while the rest seized his servants, treated them shamefully, and killed them. 7 The king was angry, and he sent his troops and destroyed those murderers and burned their city. 8 Then he said to his servants, 'The wedding is ready, but those invited were not worthy. 9 Go therefore to the thoroughfares, and invite to the marriage feast as many as you find.' 10 And those servants went out into the streets and gathered all whom they found, both bad and good; so the wedding hall was filled with guests.

11 "But when the king came in to look at the guests, he saw there a man who had no wedding garment; 12 and he said to him, 'Friend, how did you get in here without a wedding garment?' And he was speechless. 13 Then the king said to the attendants, 'Bind him hand and foot, and cast him into the outer darkness; there men will weep and gnash their teeth.' 14 For many are called, but few are chosen."

came the king sent his servants to gather all those who had been invited. The invited guests made many excuses as to why they could not come. Some even beat up and killed the messengers. The King's anger was enormous, he sent out an army to destroy the city and kill the people.

To populate the banquet the King sent for the people of the streets of all classes to come and enjoy the party. Once more the Scribes and Pharisees saw this as a derogatory statement aimed at them.

One person who came to the wedding feast had no wedding garment. This person was a pretender trying to crash the party. This would be understood only after the followers of Jesus received the Holy Spirit.

Luke has a similar story

Matthew places this parable as part of Jesus' teaching during Holy Week. Luke has a similar story but gives us no specific time where or when the parable was spoken (Luke 14:15-24).

Remember the setting for this parable was in the Temple confines. The audience consisted of Scribes, Pharisees, and common people.

Those hearing the story would have realized at once Jesus was talking about Jerusalem and the Jewish people. After the destruction of Jerusalem, many would recall the story and see it as a prophecy.

Pharisees asked, "When is the Kingdom of God coming?"	*Pharisees asked, "When is the Kingdom of God coming?"*
Luke 17:20-21 20 Being asked by the Pharisees when the kingdom of God was coming, he answered them, "The kingdom of God is not coming with signs to be observed; 21 nor will they say, 'Lo, here it is!' or 'here!' for behold, the kingdom of God is in the midst of you."	**Luke 17:20-21** **Comment** The Pharisees' concept of the kingdom of God was a domain ruled by a theocracy. They expected to be part of the ruling gentry. Jesus' concept of the kingdom of God was not a place or a thing it was a way of life. This new life would be lived out in compliance with God's will for humanity.
Pharisees and Herodians team up to discredit Jesus **Mark 12:13-17; Matthew 22:15-22; Luke 20:19-26**	*Pharisees and Herodians team up to discredit Jesus* **Mark 12:13-17; Matthew 22:15-22; Luke 20:19-26**
Mark 12:13-17 13 And they sent to him some of the Pharisees and some of the Hero'di-ans, to entrap him in	**Comment** Mark, Matthew, and Luke contain this story with little dissimilarity.

his talk. 14 And they came and said to him, "Teacher, we know that you are true, and care for no man; for you do not regard the position of men, but truly teach the way of God. Is it lawful to pay taxes to Caesar, or not? 15 Should we pay them, or should we not?" But knowing their hypocrisy, he said to them, "Why put me to the test? Bring me a coin, and let me look at it." 16 And they brought one. And he said to them, "Whose likeness and inscription is this?" They said to him, "Caesar's." 17 Jesus said to them, "Render to Caesar the things that are Caesar's, and to God the things that are God's." And they were amazed at him.

Matthew 22:15-22
15 Then the Pharisees went and took counsel how to entangle him in his talk. 16 And they sent their disciples to him, along with the Hero'di-ans, saying, "Teacher, we know that you are true, and teach the way of God truthfully, and care for no man; for you do not regard the position of men. 17 Tell us, then, what you think. Is it lawful to pay taxes to Caesar, or not?" 18 But Jesus, aware of their malice, said, "Why put me to the test, you hypocrites? 19 Show me the money for the tax." And they brought him a coin. 20 And Jesus said to them, "Whose likeness and inscription is

The Pharisees and Herodians constructed devious questions intended to ensnare Jesus. If his answer was do not pay the taxes it would bring down the wrath of the Roman conqueror. If he said pay the taxes, it would be seen as a violation of the teachings of Moses. To willingly pay the tax would be to recognize Caesar as Lord.

Jesus called for a coin. They acknowledged the likeness imprinted on it was that of Caesar. Jesus' response was more powerful than the words would simply indicate. Material things belong to the material world. Spiritual things belong to the realm of God.

this?" 21 They said, "Caesar's." Then he said to them, "Render therefore to Caesar the things that are Caesar's, and to God the things that are God's." 22 When they heard it, they marveled; and they left him and went away.

Luke 20:19-26

19 The scribes and the chief priests tried to lay hands on him at that very hour, but they feared the people; for they perceived that he had told this parable against them. 20 So they watched him, and sent spies, who pretended to be sincere, that they might take hold of what he said, so as to deliver him up to the authority and jurisdiction of the governor. 21 They asked him, "Teacher, we know that you speak and teach rightly, and show no partiality, but truly teach the way of God. 22 Is it lawful for us to give tribute to Caesar, or not?" 23 But he perceived their craftiness, and said to them, 24 "Show me a coin. Whose likeness and inscription has it?" They said, "Caesar's." 25 He said to them, "Then render to Caesar the things that are Caesar's, and to God the things that are God's." 26 And they were not able in the presence of the people to catch him by what he said; but marveling at his answer they were silent.

Sadducees try to discredit Jesus

Mark 12:18-27;
Matthew 22:23-33;
Luke 20:27-40

Mark 12:18-27

18 And Sad'ducees came to him, who say that there is no resurrection; and they asked him a question, saying, 19 "Teacher, Moses wrote for us that if a man's brother dies and leaves a wife, but leaves no child, the man must take the wife, and raise up children for his brother. 20 There were seven brothers; the first took a wife, and when he died left no children; 21 and the second took her, and died, leaving no children; and the third likewise; 22 and the seven left no children. Last of all the woman also died. 23 In the resurrection whose wife will she be? For the seven had her as wife."

24 Jesus said to them, "Is not this why you are wrong, that you know neither the scriptures nor the power of God? 25 For when they rise from the dead, they neither marry nor are given in marriage, but are like angels in heaven. 26 And as for the dead being raised, have you not read in the book of Moses, in the passage about the bush, how God said to him, 'I am the God of Abraham, and the God of Isaac, and the

Sadducees try to discredit Jesus

Mark 12:18-27;
Matthew 22:23-33;
Luke 20:27-40

Comment

The Sadducees did not believe there would be a resurrection of the dead. So they posed a preposterous question. Their question involved a widow of seven brothers. They based their question on Deuteronomy chapter 25.

If brothers dwell together, and one of them dies and has no son, the wife of the dead shall not be married outside the family to a stranger; her husband's brother shall go in to her, and take her as his wife, and perform the duty of a husband's brother to her. – Deuteronomy 25:5

Jesus gave them a devastating response. He told them within the hearing of the crowd that they knew nothing about the Scripture or the power of God.

Jesus' response can be disquieting to some. Jesus said marriage as we know it will not exist after the resurrection. Many wish Jesus had said that earthly marriages would continue in heaven.

God of Jacob'? 27 He is not God of the dead, but of the living; you are quite wrong."

Matthew 22:23-33
23 The same day Sad'ducees came to him, who say that there is no resurrection; and they asked him a question, 24 saying, "Teacher, Moses said, 'If a man dies, having no children, his brother must marry the widow, and raise up children for his brother.' 25 Now there were seven brothers among us; the first married, and died, and having no children left his wife to his brother. 26 So too the second and third, down to the seventh. 27 After them all, the woman died. 28 In the resurrection, therefore, to which of the seven will she be wife? For they all had her." 29 But Jesus answered them, "You are wrong, because you know neither the scriptures nor the power of God. 30 For in the resurrection they neither marry nor are given in marriage, but are like angels in heaven. 31 And as for the resurrection of the dead, have you not read what was said to you by God, 32 'I am the God of Abraham, and the God of Isaac, and the God of Jacob'? He is not God of the dead, but of the living." 33 And when the crowd heard it, they were astonished at his teaching.

Jesus answered the question of what we will be like after the resurrection. The resurrected will be like angels. Not like humans.

Luke 20:27-40

27 There came to him some Sadducees, those who say that there is no resurrection, 28 and they asked him a question, saying, "Teacher, Moses wrote for us that if a man's brother dies, having a wife but no children, the man must take the wife and raise up children for his brother. 29 Now there were seven brothers; the first took a wife, and died without children; 30 and the second 31 and the third took her, and likewise all seven left no children and died. 32 Afterward the woman also died. 33 In the resurrection, therefore, whose wife will the woman be? For the seven had her as wife."

34 And Jesus said to them, "The sons of this age marry and are given in marriage; 35 but those who are accounted worthy to attain to that age and to the resurrection from the dead neither marry nor are given in marriage, 36 for they cannot die any more, because they are equal to angels and are sons of God, being sons of the resurrection. 37 But that the dead are raised, even Moses showed, in the passage about the bush, where he calls the Lord the God of Abraham and the God of Isaac and the God of Jacob. 38 Now he is not God of the dead, but of the living; for all live to him." 39 And some of the scribes answered, "Teacher,

you have spoken well." [40] For they no longer dared to ask him any question.

Scribes try to discredit Jesus

**Mark 12:28-34;
Matthew 22:34-40**

Mark 12:28-34

[28] And one of the scribes came up and heard them disputing with one another, and seeing that he answered them well, asked him, "Which commandment is the first of all?" [29] Jesus answered, "The first is, 'Hear, O Israel: The Lord our God, the Lord is one; [30] and you shall love the Lord your God with all your heart, and with all your soul, and with all your mind, and with all your strength.' [31] The second is this, 'You shall love your neighbor as yourself.' There is no other commandment greater than these." [32] And the scribe said to him, "You are right, Teacher; you have truly said that he is one, and there is no other but he; [33] and to love him with all the heart, and with all the understanding, and with all the strength, and to love one's neighbor as oneself, is much more than all whole burnt offerings and sacrifices." [34] And when Jesus saw that he answered wisely, he said to him, "You are not far from the kingdom of God." And after that no one dared to ask him any question.

Scribes try to discredit Jesus

**Mark 12:28-34;
Matthew 22:34-40**

Comment

The reference is to a section known as the Shema, found in Deuteronomy 6:4-9. This is not one of the Ten Commandments given to Moses.

The titles of scribe and lawyer were interchangeable during Jesus' time. Jesus responded to the comment by saying, "You are near the kingdom of God." He did not say that he was there yet. Why? Perhaps there was a gap existing between his knowledge and his lifestyle.

Matthew 22:34-40
34 But when the Pharisees heard that he had silenced the Sad'ducees, they came together. 35 And one of them, a lawyer, asked him a question, to test him. 36 "Teacher, which is the great commandment in the law?" 37 And he said to him, "You shall love the Lord your God with all your heart, and with all your soul, and with all your mind. 38 This is the great and first commandment. 39 And a second is like it, You shall love your neighbor as yourself. 40 On these two commandments depend all the law and the prophets."

Jesus says, Woe unto you …
Scribes and Pharisees,
hypocrites!

Matthew 23:13-15
13 "But woe to you, scribes and Pharisees, hypocrites! because you shut the kingdom of heaven against men; for you neither enter yourselves, nor allow those who would enter to go in. 15 Woe to you, scribes and Pharisees, hypocrites! for you traverse sea and land to make a single proselyte, and when he becomes a proselyte, you make him twice as much a child of hell as yourselves."

Jesus says, Woe unto you …
Scribes and Pharisees,
hypocrites!

Matthew 23:13-15

Comment
Jesus labeled the scribes and Pharisees as hypocrites; play actors. He devastatingly said to them they shut the doors of the kingdom, rather than opening them. He said they were not going to enter the kingdom, and they were preventing others from entering. Verse fifteen could be interpreted to say the non-believer is a child of hell.

Jesus blistered all the ranks of spiritual leadership

Jesus blistered the spiritual leadership of his time: the rulers, priests, Sadducees, zealous Pharisees, and the learned scribes.

Blind guides

Matthew 23:16-22

16 "Woe to you, blind guides, who say, 'If any one swears by the temple, it is nothing; but if any one swears by the gold of the temple, he is bound by his oath.' 17 You blind fools! For which is greater, the gold or the temple that has made the gold sacred? 18 And you say, 'If any one swears by the altar, it is nothing; but if any one swears by the gift that is on the altar, he is bound by his oath.' 19 You blind men! For which is greater, the gift or the altar that makes the gift sacred? 20 So he who swears by the altar, swears by it and by everything on it; 21 and he who swears by the temple, swears by it and by him who dwells in it; 22 and he who swears by heaven, swears by the throne of God and by him who sits upon it.

Swallow a camel!

Matthew 23:23-24

23 "Woe to you, scribes and Pharisees, hypocrites! for you tithe mint and dill and cummin, and have neglected the weightier

---

Blind guides

Comment

Matthew 23:16-22

Here Jesus spoke to the issue of oaths. Jesus said if you make an oath invoking the Temple or the altar it is binding. But the greater thing is if one makes an oath swearing to heaven he is swearing to God.

In the ancient world an oath was a very serious matter, it was today's equivalent of a notarized contract. One who gave an oath was compelled to fulfill that oath, or run the risk of Divine intervention and retribution.

Swallow a camel!

Matthew 23:23-24

Comment

The subject here is the tithe. Jesus accused the scribes and

matters of the law, justice and mercy and faith; these you ought to have done, without neglecting the others. 24 You blind guides, straining out a gnat and swallowing a camel!

Pharisees of being hypocrites because they paid attention to the small matters while neglecting the more important ones. They were scrupulous in paying the tithe on small items such as the spices, dill and cumin. Jesus went on to say they neglect the weightier or more important matters of the tithe, the law, justice, mercy, and faith. These elements they omitted from their lives, and teaching. He said their teaching was like someone straining out a gnat, while at the same time swallowing a camel.

Whitewashed tombs

Whitewashed tombs

Matthew 23:25-28

Matthew 23:25-28

25 "Woe to you, scribes and Pharisees, hypocrites! for you cleanse the outside of the cup and of the plate, but inside they are full of extortion and rapacity. 26 You blind Pharisee! first cleanse the inside of the cup and of the plate, that the outside also may be clean.27 "Woe to you, scribes and Pharisees, hypocrites! for you are like whitewashed tombs, which outwardly appear beautiful, but within they are full of dead men's bones and all uncleanness. 28 So you also outwardly appear righteous to men, but within you are full of hypocrisy and iniquity.

Comment

Here the issue is being clean, or unclean. Jesus illustrated this by using a cup and a plate as representative objects. He said the cup can be clean on the outside and filthy on the inside. Likewise, the person may appear to be the epitome of goodness on the outside, while their heart may be filled with deceit, villainy, and corruption. He told the scribes and the Pharisees to cleanse their inner being and then they would be seen as they wanted people to view them.

Matthew 23:27-28 is the same concept, except using a tomb rather than a cup and a plate.

You brood of vipers

Matthew 23:29-36

29 "Woe to you, scribes and Pharisees, hypocrites! for you build the tombs of the prophets and adorn the monuments of the righteous, 30 saying, 'If we had lived in the days of our fathers, we would not have taken part with them in shedding the blood of the prophets.' 31 Thus you witness against yourselves, that you are sons of those who murdered the prophets. 32 Fill up, then, the measure of your fathers. 33 You serpents, you brood of vipers, how are you to escape being sentenced to hell? 34 Therefore I send you prophets and wise men and scribes, some of whom you will kill and crucify, and some you will scourge in your synagogues and persecute from town to town, 35 that upon you may come all the righteous blood shed on earth, from the blood of innocent Abel to the blood of Zechari'ah the son of Barachi'ah, whom you murdered between the sanctuary and the altar. 36 Truly, I say to you, all this will come upon this generation.

You brood of vipers

Matthew 23:29-36

Comment

Here the subject is the killing of the prophets and condemning those who offer understanding of God's Word that differs from the accepted doctrines of the scribes, Pharisees and Sadducees.

Jesus went on to call them a brood of vipers. What a repulsive description of people, regardless of how high and mighty they may consider themselves. Jesus said all the innocent blood that had been shed from the time of Abel until the present time rested upon people such as them who consider themselves more righteous than any other, who would go to any length to enforce their interpretations of the law and their doctrines.

Jesus Laments for Jerusalem	*Jesus Laments for Jerusalem*
Matthew 23:37-39; **Luke 13:34-35**	**Matthew 23:37-39;** **Luke 13:34-35**

Matthew 23:37-39

37 "O Jerusalem, Jerusalem, killing the prophets and stoning those who are sent to you! How often would I have gathered your children together as a hen gathers her brood under her wings, and you would not! 38 Behold, your house is forsaken and desolate. 39 For I tell you, you will not see me again, until you say, 'Blessed is he who comes in the name of the Lord.'"

Luke 13:34-35

34 O Jerusalem, Jerusalem, killing the prophets and stoning those who are sent to you! How often would I have gathered your children together as a hen gathers her brood under her wings, and you would not! 35 Behold, your house is forsaken. And I tell you, you will not see me until you say, 'Blessed is he who comes in the name of the Lord!'"

Comment

Jesus recalled the history of Jerusalem and its handling of the prophets who brought word from God. Jerusalem had a bloody history of dealings with the prophets. Jesus passed judgment on Jerusalem for this history.

Jesus' illustration of the hen is a kind and compassionate statement, perhaps inspired by Psalms 91:4.
he will cover you with his pinions, and under his wings you will find refuge; his faithfulness is a shield and buckler.

Jerusalem will become desolate, the word also means: solitary, lonely, uninhabited, cut of from the aid and protection of others, especially of friends, acquaintances, kindred; like a flock, deserted by the shepherd.

On Monday of Holy Week the crowd had shouted "Blessed is he who comes in the name of the Lord." (Mark 11:9)

Jesus quoted 2 Chronicles chapter 24

20 Then the Spirit of God took possession of Zechari'ah the son of Jehoi'ada the priest; and he stood above the people, and said to them, "Thus says God, 'Why do you transgress the commandments of the LORD, so that you cannot prosper? Because you have forsaken the LORD, he has forsaken you.'" 21 But they conspired against him, and by command of the king they stoned him with stones in the court of the house of the LORD.
– 2 Chronicles 24:20-21

Jeremiah 26:20-23 provides another.

20 There was another man who prophesied in the name of the LORD, Uri'ah the son of Shemai'ah from Kir'iath-je'arim. He prophesied against this city and against this land in words like those of Jeremiah. 21 And when King Jehoi'akim, with all his warriors and all the princes, heard his words, the king sought to put him to death; but when Uri'ah heard of it, he was afraid and fled and escaped to Egypt. 22 Then King Jehoi'akim sent to Egypt certain men, Elna'than the son of Achbor and others with him, 23 and they fetched Uri'ah from Egypt and brought him to King Jehoi'akim, who slew him with the sword and cast his dead body into the burial place of the common people.

Jesus faces them down	*Jesus faces them down*
Mark 12:35-40; Matthew 22:41-46; Luke 20:41-47	Mark 12:35-40; Matthew 22:41-46; Luke 20:41-47
Mark 12:35-40 35 And as Jesus taught in the temple, he said, "How can the scribes say that the Christ is the son of David? 36 David himself, inspired by the Holy Spirit, declared, 'The Lord said to my Lord, Sit at my right hand, till I put thy enemies under thy feet.' 37 David himself calls him Lord; so how is he his son?" And the	**Comment** While teaching Jesus asked a specific question concerning King David, "How can the scribes say that the Christ is the son of David?" Jesus quotes from Psalms 110: 1; "The Lord said to my Lord." Thus postulating David would not have called his son "Lord."

great throng heard him gladly. 38 And in his teaching he said, "Beware of the scribes, who like to go about in long robes, and to have salutations in the market places 39 and the best seats in the synagogues and the places of honor at feasts, 40 who devour widows' houses and for a pretense make long prayers. They will receive the greater condemnation."

Matthew 22:41-46
41 Now while the Pharisees were gathered together, Jesus asked them a question, 42 saying, "What do you think of the Christ? Whose son is he?" They said to him, "The son of David." 43 He said to them, "How is it then that David, inspired by the Spirit, calls him Lord, saying,
44 'The Lord said to my Lord, Sit at my right hand, till I put thy enemies under thy feet'?
45 If David thus calls him Lord, how is he his son?" 46 And no one was able to answer him a word, nor from that day did any one dare to ask him any more questions.

Luke 20:41-47
41 But he said to them, "How can they say that the Christ is David's son? 42 For David himself says in the Book of Psalms,
'The Lord said to my Lord, Sit at my right hand,
43 till I make thy enemies a stool

Who are the scribes? Scribes were experts in the Law of Moses. The significance of long robes that touched the ground was they were a sign of nobility and wealth. Long robes were not intended for a working person. Undoubtedly such attire would draw attention to the person. The scribes loved to be greeted as Rabbi, which can mean "my great one."

To sit in front facing the congregation to be seen by everyone were considered places of honor. The place of honor at a feast was to sit at the right hand of the host.

Experts in the law could not accept any pay for their teaching. In many instances however they were able to communicate that there was a higher law. This higher law would accept "gifts" in lieu of an outright payment. Scribes and Pharisees were notorious for their long prayers.

Matthew said Jesus asked a direct question of the Pharisees concerning David. He frequently asked a question by way of answering a question. Matthew closes with a statement that no one dared ask Jesus any questions after this.

for thy feet.'
44 David thus calls him Lord; so how is he his son?"
45 And in the hearing of all the people he said to his disciples, 46 "Beware of the scribes, who like to go about in long robes, and love salutations in the market places and the best seats in the synagogues and the places of honor at feasts, 47 who devour widows' houses and for a pretense make long prayers. They will receive the greater condemnation."

Moses' seat

Matthew 23:1-12
1 Then said Jesus to the crowds and to his disciples, 2 "The scribes and the Pharisees sit on Moses' seat; 3 so practice and observe whatever they tell you, but not what they do; for they preach, but do not practice. 4 They bind heavy burdens, hard to bear, and lay them on men's shoulders; but they themselves will not move them with their finger. 5 They do all their deeds to be seen by men; for they make their phylacteries broad and their fringes long, 6 and they love the place of honor at feasts and the best seats in the synagogues, 7 and salutations in the market places, and being called rabbi by men. 8 But you are not to be called rabbi, for you

Moses' seat

Matthew 23:1-12

Comment
"Moses seat" was the preeminent spot in the synagogue. The seat of Moses was reserved for special guest speakers. Jesus draws a hard distinction between what the scribes and Pharisees teach and how they live. He told his listeners and especially the Inner-Circle to do what they say, but do not do what they do. The burdens they create are hard for men to carry. Jesus told his followers not to seek acclaim for themselves nor call any earthly being father for their Father is in heaven.

have one teacher, and you are all brethren. [9] And call no man your father on earth, for you have one Father, who is in heaven. [10] Neither be called masters, for you have one master, the Christ. [11] He who is greatest among you shall be your servant; [12] whoever exalts himself will be humbled, and whoever humbles himself will be exalted.

Widow's two copper coins

Mark 12:41-44;
Luke 21:1-4

Mark 12:41-44
[41] And he sat down opposite the treasury, and watched the multitude putting money into the treasury. Many rich people put in large sums.
[42] And a poor widow came, and put in two copper coins, which make a penny.
[43] And he called his disciples to him, and said to them, "Truly, I say to you, this poor widow has put in more than all those who are contributing to the treasury.
[44] For they all contributed out of their abundance; but she out of her poverty has put in everything she had, her whole living."

Luke 21:1-4
[1] He looked up and saw the rich putting their gifts into the treasury;
[2] and he saw a poor widow put in

Widow's two copper coins

Mark 12:41-44
Luke 21:1-4

Comment
In the court of the women there were thirteen collection boxes called the trumpets, because of their shape. Each box was for a special purpose.

Frequently the rich would hire a trumpeter to sound a blast from the trumpet as they dropped their offerings in the collection box.

Copper coins were the smallest denomination of currency available.

Money is very important to everyone. The less you have the more important it becomes. For this poor widow God was more important than all the money she possessed!

two copper coins. 3 And he said, "Truly I tell you, this poor widow has put in more than all of them; 4 for they all contributed out of their abundance, but she out of her poverty put in all the living that she had."

Whatever the disciples were doing, they certainly were not paying attention to this widow as she gave her offering.

Here is the clearest statement Jesus gave concerning ones giving of their financial wealth to God. Without question Jesus is lifting up percentage giving.

Chapter 5

Holy Week: Wednesday Afternoon

Jesus leaves the Temple	*Jesus leaves the Temple*
Mark 13:1-2; Matthew 24:1-2; Luke 21:5-6	Mark 13:1-2; Matthew 24:1-2; Luke 21:5-6

Mark 13:1-2

^{1} And as he came out of the temple, one of his disciples said to him, "Look, Teacher, what wonderful stones and what wonderful buildings!" ^{2} And Jesus said to him, "Do you see these great buildings? There will not be left here one stone upon another, that will not be thrown down."

Matthew 24:1-2

^{1} Jesus left the temple and was going away, when his disciples came to point out to him the buildings of the temple. ^{2} But he answered them, "You see all these, do you not? Truly, I say to you, there will not be left here one stone upon another, that will not be thrown down."

Luke 21:5-6

^{5} And as some spoke of the temple, how it was adorned with noble stones and offerings, he said, ^{6} "As for these things which you see, the days will

Comment

Jesus led the Inner-Circle from the temple; it had been a long day. Looking at their surroundings they called his attention to the wonderful stones and beautiful buildings. Jesus then told them that the time was coming when there would not be one stone left upon another.

come when there shall not be left here one stone upon another that will not be thrown down."

Jesus speaks of the end times

Mark 13:3-8;
Matthew 24:3-8;
Luke 21:7-11

Mark 13:3-8
3 And as he sat on the Mount of Olives opposite the temple, Peter and James and John and Andrew asked him privately, 4 "Tell us, when will this be, and what will be the sign when these things are all to be accomplished?" 5 And Jesus began to say to them, "Take heed that no one leads you astray. 6 Many will come in my name, saying, 'I am he!' and they will lead many astray. 7 And when you hear of wars and rumors of wars, do not be alarmed; this must take place, but the end is not yet. 8 For nation will rise against nation, and kingdom against kingdom; there will be earthquakes in various places, there will be famines; this is but the beginning of the birth-pangs.

Matthew 24:3-8
3 As he sat on the Mount of Olives, the disciples came to him privately, saying, "Tell us, when will this be, and what will be the sign of your coming and of the close of the age?" 4 And Jesus answered them, "Take heed that

Jesus speaks of the end times

Mark 13:3-8;
Matthew 24:3-8;
Luke 21:7-11

Comment
The Inner-Circle was anxious to know when this would happen. Jesus told them the signs they would see would be pretenders coming in his name, claiming to be the Christ. They would hear rumors of war, nation would rise against nation. There would be famine and earthquake in various parts of the world. But all of these would be just the prelude to the impending disaster.

no one leads you astray. 5 For many will come in my name, saying, 'I am the Christ,' and they will lead many astray. 6 And you will hear of wars and rumors of wars; see that you are not alarmed; for this must take place, but the end is not yet. 7 For nation will rise against nation, and kingdom against kingdom, and there will be famines and earthquakes in various places: 8 all this is but the beginning of the birth-pangs.

Luke 21:7-11

5 And as some spoke of the temple, how it was adorned with noble stones and offerings, he said, 6 "As for these things which you see, the days will come when there shall not be left here one stone upon another that will not be thrown down." 7 And they asked him, "Teacher, when will this be, and what will be the sign when this is about to take place?" 8 And he said, "Take heed that you are not led astray; for many will come in my name, saying, 'I am he!' and, 'The time is at hand!' Do not go after them. 9 And when you hear of wars and tumults, do not be terrified; for this must first take place, but the end will not be at once." 10 Then he said to them, "Nation will rise against nation, and kingdom against kingdom; 11 there will be great earthquakes, and in various

places famines and pestilences; and there will be terrors and great signs from heaven.

Tribulation

**Mark 13:9-13;
Matthew 24:9-14;
Luke 21:12-19**

Mark 13:9-13

9 "But take heed to yourselves; for they will deliver you up to councils; and you will be beaten in synagogues; and you will stand before governors and kings for my sake, to bear testimony before them. 10 And the gospel must first be preached to all nations. 11 And when they bring you to trial and deliver you up, do not be anxious beforehand what you are to say; but say whatever is given you in that hour, for it is not you who speak, but the Holy Spirit. 12 And brother will deliver up brother to death, and the father his child, and children will rise against parents and have them put to death; 13 and you will be hated by all for my name's sake. But he who endures to the end will be saved.

Matthew 24:9-14

9 "Then they will deliver you up to tribulation, and put you to death; and you will be hated by all nations for my name's sake. 10 And then many will fall away,

Tribulation

**Mark 13:9-13;
Matthew 24:9-14;
Luke 21:12-19**

Comment

Jesus told the Inner-Circle the way would be hard and there would be many dangers and problems. He warned them they would be compelled to stand before councils, Governors, and Kings. Some would endure beatings in synagogues, because they held fast their faith in him. He said to them, "When these authorities call you to give your witness do not worry about what you are going to say, because the Holy Spirit will give you his word to speak." Wickedness would run rampant during this period and many would fall away but the gospel of the kingdom would be preached throughout the whole world. After this the end would come.

and betray one another, and hate one another. 11 And many false prophets will arise and lead many astray. 12 And because wickedness is multiplied, most men's love will grow cold. 13 But he who endures to the end will be saved. 14 And this gospel of the kingdom will be preached throughout the whole world, as a testimony to all nations; and then the end will come.

Luke 21:12-19

12 But before all this they will lay their hands on you and persecute you, delivering you up to the synagogues and prisons, and you will be brought before kings and governors for my name's sake. 13 This will be a time for you to bear testimony. 14 Settle it therefore in your minds, not to meditate beforehand how to answer; 15 for I will give you a mouth and wisdom, which none of your adversaries will be able to withstand or contradict. 16 You will be delivered up even by parents and brothers and kinsmen and friends, and some of you they will put to death; 17 you will be hated by all for my name's sake. 18 But not a hair of your head will perish. 19 By your endurance you will gain your lives.

When the persecutions did come

James, the brother of John, was among the first to die.
1Herod the king laid violent hands upon some who belonged to the church.2 He killed James the brother of John with the sword; – Acts 12:1-2

James, the brother of Jesus (Matt. 13:55), was martyred by the scribes and Pharisees who threw him from the pinnacle of the Temple. When the fall did not kill him they began to stone him. Finally they beat him with a club. (Lockyer, Herbert. *All the Men of the Bible*, page 171.)

The Apostle Paul would stand before Governors, Kings, and councils and in the end pay with his life for his faithfulness.
13 Now when some days had passed, Agrippa the king and Bernice arrived at Caesare'a to welcome Festus. 14 And as they stayed there many days, Festus laid Paul's case before the king, saying, "There is a man left prisoner by Felix; 15 and when I was at Jerusalem, the chief priests and the elders of the Jews gave information about him, asking for sentence against him." – Acts 25:13-15

Peter would follow something of the same path. Peter was executed in Rome in 61 A.D. Tradition tells us that he was crucified upside down feeling that he was unworthy to die in the exact position of the Lord Jesus Christ. (Lockyer, Herbert. *All the Men of the Bible*, page 273.)

Desolating sacrilege	*Desolating sacrilege*
Mark 13:14-23; **Matthew 24:15-28;** **Luke 21:20-24**	**Mark 13:14-23;** **Matthew 24:15-28;** **Luke 21:20-24**
Mark 13:14-23 14 "But when you see the desolating sacrilege set up where it ought not to be (let the reader understand), then let those who are in Judea flee to the mountains; 15 let him who is on the housetop not go down, nor	**Comment** Both Mark and Matthew include, "(let the reader understand)". This is likely a later addition to the original text by a scribe.

enter his house, to take anything away; 16 and let him who is in the field not turn back to take his mantle. 17 And alas for those who are with child and for those who give suck in those days! 18 Pray that it may not happen in winter. 19 For in those days there will be such tribulation as has not been from the beginning of the creation which God created until now, and never will be. 20 And if the Lord had not shortened the days, no human being would be saved; but for the sake of the elect, whom he chose, he shortened the days. 21 And then if any one says to you, 'Look, here is the Christ!' or 'Look, there he is!' do not believe it. 22 False Christs and false prophets will arise and show signs and wonders, to lead astray, if possible, the elect. 23 But take heed; I have told you all things beforehand.

Matthew 24:15-28
15 "So when you see the desolating sacrilege spoken of by the prophet Daniel, standing in the holy place (let the reader understand), 16 then let those who are in Judea flee to the mountains; 17 let him who is on the housetop not go down to take what is in his house; 18 and let him who is in the field not turn back to take his mantle. 19 And alas for those who are with child and for those who give suck in

Jesus' warnings may be seen in one of two ways. It could have been a short-term prophecy of the destruction of Jerusalem, or a long-term prophecy yet to be fulfilled.

Jesus warned against remaining in Jerusalem or Judea. His advice was to flee to the hills, which could mean Galilee or the Decapolis. When the end of Jerusalem came in 70 A.D. the people did just the opposite.

They came from all over the country and flooded into the city of Jerusalem. Ultimately most were slaughtered in the assaults upon the city by Roman Legions.

The word translated, desolation means total destruction. The word sacrilege probably refers to the conqueror setting up images of false gods in the very precincts of the Holy of Holies.

Mark said this tribulation would be greater than anything that had ever struck the earth before or would ever strike it again. To the Jewish mind, nothing could be greater than the destruction of the Temple and the city of Jerusalem. The days of tribulation would be shortened for the sake of the elect, those who had chosen to be followers of Jesus Christ.

those days! 20 Pray that your flight may not be in winter or on a sabbath. 21 For then there will be great tribulation, such as has not been from the beginning of the world until now, no, and never will be. 22 And if those days had not been shortened, no human being would be saved; but for the sake of the elect those days will be shortened. 23 Then if any one says to you, 'Lo, here is the Christ!' or 'There he is!' do not believe it. 24 For false Christs and false prophets will arise and show great signs and wonders, so as to lead astray, if possible, even the elect. 25 Lo, I have told you beforehand. 26 So, if they say to you, 'Lo, he is in the wilderness,' do not go out; if they say, 'Lo, he is in the inner rooms,' do not believe it. 27 For as the lightning comes from the east and shines as far as the west, so will be the coming of the Son of man. 28 Wherever the body is, there the eagles will be gathered together.

Luke 21:20-24

20 "But when you see Jerusalem surrounded by armies, then know that its desolation has come near. 21 Then let those who are in Judea flee to the mountains, and let those who are inside the city distress shall be upon the earth and wrath upon this people; 24 they will fall by the edge of the

Jesus again warned not to follow false Christs or false prophets for they would do many signs and wonders but these were designed to deceive.

The situation would be so urgent one would have no time to delay. If they were on the housetop they were not to take time to go downstairs and gather their belongings.

He admonished the people to pray that the desolating sacrilege not happen in the wintertime or on a Sabbath. In wintertime food supplies could become very short and very hard to obtain. The laws of the Sabbath prohibited a journey of any length necessary for safety.

sword, and be led captive among all nations; and Jerusalem will be trodden down by the Gentiles, until the times of the Gentiles are fulfilled.	

Jesus makes references from the book of Daniel

And he shall make a strong covenant with many for one week; and for half of the week he shall cause sacrifice and offering to cease; and upon the wing of abominations shall come one who makes desolate, until the decreed end is poured out on the desolator.
– Daniel 9:27

Forces from him shall appear and profane the temple and fortress, and shall take away the continual burnt offering. And they shall set up the abomination that makes desolate. – Daniel 11:31

And from the time that the continual burnt offering is taken away, and the abomination that makes desolate is set up, there shall be a thousand two hundred and ninety days.
– Daniel 12:11

Luke clarifies the situation

Luke defines these days as days of vengeance. He clarifies the situation to some extent saying, they would see armies surrounding Jerusalem which would be a sign that the desolation was very near.

Josephus in his book, *The Wars of the Jews*, states that 97,000 people were taken captive and another 1,100,000 died of starvation and the sword in Jerusalem.

Jerusalem would be destroyed by gentiles and overrun by them until their time was fulfilled. This is an obscure statement and difficult to define. The Arabic nations would be considered as gentiles. Palestinian Arabs occupied Jerusalem for centuries. The new state of Israel was legislated in 1947 by the United Nations.

After the Tribulation	*After the Tribulation*
Mark 13:24-27; **Matthew 24:29-31;** **Luke 21:25-28**	**Mark 13:24-27;** **Matthew 24:29-31;** **Luke 21:25-28**
Mark 13:24-27 24 "But in those days, after that tribulation, the sun will be darkened, and the moon will not give its light, 25 and the stars will be falling from heaven, and the powers in the heavens will be shaken. 26 And then they will see the Son of man coming in clouds with great power and glory. 27 And then he will send out the angels, and gather his elect from the four winds, from the ends of the earth to the ends of heaven. **Matthew 24:29-31** 29 "Immediately after the tribulation of those days the sun will be darkened, and the moon will not give its light, and the stars will fall from heaven, and the powers of the heavens will be shaken; 30 then will appear the sign of the Son of man in heaven, and then all the tribes of the earth will mourn, and they will see the Son of man coming on the clouds of heaven with power and great glory; 31 and he will send out his angels with a loud trumpet call, and they will gather his elect from the four winds, from one end of heaven to the other.	**Comment** The description Jesus gave of the aftermath of the tribulation is reminiscent of the effects of modern warfare. The effects of bombing and artillery send up clouds of dirt and smoke that hang over an area for an extended period of time before it dissipates. Whatever else may be said about this statement, one fact is absolutely true, the moon reflects light from the sun. Therefore, if the sun is darkened, there will be no source of light for the moon. Should all the distant suns become darkened, it would appear that all of the stars would have fallen out of the sky. Out of the cosmic chaos will be heard a trumpet blast and the Son of God will appear on the clouds. This passage sounds to me as though it could have been taken straight from Daniel or Revelation. Personally, I have difficulty reconciling this passage with the gentle love of Jesus Christ.

Luke 21:25-28

25 "And there will be signs in sun and moon and stars, and upon the earth distress of nations in perplexity at the roaring of the sea and the waves, 26 men fainting with fear and with foreboding of what is coming on the world; for the powers of the heavens will be shaken. 27 And then they will see the Son of man coming in a cloud with power and great glory. 28 Now when these things begin to take place, look up and raise your heads, because your redemption is drawing near."

Lesson from the Fig Tree

**Mark 13:28-31;
Matthew 24:32-35;
Luke 21:29-33**

Mark 13:28-31

28 "From the fig tree learn its lesson: as soon as its branch becomes tender and puts forth its leaves, you know that summer is near. 29 So also, when you see these things taking place, you know that he is near, at the very gates. 30 Truly, I say to you, this generation will not pass away before all these things take place. 31 Heaven and earth will pass away, but my words will not pass away.

Matthew 24:32-35

32 "From the fig tree learn its lesson: as soon as its branch

Lesson from the Fig Tree

**Mark 13:28-31;
Matthew 24:32-35;
Luke 21:29-33**

Comment

Matthew, Mark, and Luke begin this passage in the same way saying, "Look at the fig tree." Those listening to Jesus understood the cycle of the fig tree from dormancy of winter to the yielding of fruit in the spring. As dependable as the fig tree was, so is the word of Jesus.

The span of a generation would be considered thirty to thirty-five years. Within that span of time they would experience the catastrophe, and all that had been foretold.

becomes tender and puts forth its leaves, you know that summer is near. 33 So also, when you see all these things, you know that he is near, at the very gates. 34 Truly, I say to you, this generation will not pass away till all these things take place. 35 Heaven and earth will pass away, but my words will not pass away.

Luke 21:29-33
29 And he told them a parable: "Look at the fig tree, and all the trees; 30 as soon as they come out in leaf, you see for yourselves and know that the summer is already near. 31 So also, when you see these things taking place, you know that the kingdom of God is near. 32 Truly, I say to you, this generation will not pass away till all has taken place. 33 Heaven and earth will pass away, but my words will not pass away.

If these passages are to be understood as the destruction of Jerusalem, the time of a generation would fit almost perfectly. Jesus was approximately thirty-two years of age at his crucifixion and approximately thirty-eight years later the city of Jerusalem was destroyed by the Romans.

No one knows when

**Mark 13:32-37;
Matthew 24:36-44;
Luke 21:34-36**

No one knows when

**Mark 13:32-37;
Matthew 24:36-44;
Luke 21:34-36**

Mark 13:32-37
32 "But of that day or that hour no one knows, not even the angels in heaven, nor the Son, but only the Father. 33 Take heed, watch; for you do not know when the time will come. 34 It is like a man going on a journey, when he leaves home and puts his servants

Comment
Jesus made the point that no one knew the time for his return. He illustrated this by saying a man went on a journey and left all of his business in the hands of his employees. They were ordered to watch for the man's return. (Parable of the Talents, Matt. 25:14ff.)

in charge, each with his work, and commands the doorkeeper to be on the watch. 35 Watch therefore -- for you do not know when the master of the house will come, in the evening, or at midnight, or at cockcrow, or in the morning -- 36 lest he come suddenly and find you asleep. 37 And what I say to you I say to all: Watch."

Matthew 24:36-44
36 "But of that day and hour no one knows, not even the angels of heaven, nor the Son, but the Father only. 37 As were the days of Noah, so will be the coming of the Son of man. 38 For as in those days before the flood they were eating and drinking, marrying and giving in marriage, until the day when Noah entered the ark, 39 and they did not know until the flood came and swept them all away, so will be the coming of the Son of man. 40 Then two men will be in the field; one is taken and one is left. 41 Two women will be grinding at the mill; one is taken and one is left. 42 Watch therefore, for you do not know on what day your Lord is coming. 43 But know this, that if the householder had known in what part of the night the thief was coming, he would have watched and would not have let his house be broken into. 44 Therefore you also must be ready; for the Son of man is coming at an hour you

Matthew adds two additional emphases: two men working in the field, two women grinding at a mill; in each case one is taken and one is left. Had each of these known the moment of their visitation all would have been prepared. Since none know the moment of this occurrence all must remain alert and prepared.

God said to Ezekiel, *17 "Son of man, I have made you a watchman for the house of Israel; whenever you hear a word from my mouth, you shall give them warning from me. 18 If I say to the wicked, 'You shall surely die,' and you give him no warning, nor speak to warn the wicked from his wicked way, in order to save his life, that wicked man shall die in his iniquity; but his blood I will require at your hand. 19 But if you warn the wicked, and he does not turn from his wickedness, or from his wicked way, he shall die in his iniquity; but you will have saved your life. 20 Again, if a righteous man turns from his righteousness and commits iniquity, and I lay a stumbling block before him, he shall die; because you have not warned him, he shall die for his sin, and his righteous deeds which he has done shall not be remembered; but his blood I will require at your hand.*
– Ezekiel 3:17-20

do not expect.

Luke 21:34-36
34 "But take heed to yourselves lest your hearts be weighed down with dissipation and drunkenness and cares of this life, and that day come upon you suddenly like a snare; 35 for it will come upon all who dwell upon the face of the whole earth. 36 But watch at all times, praying that you may have strength to escape all these things that will take place, and to stand before the Son of man."

Remain faithful

Matthew 24:45-51
45 "Who then is the faithful and wise servant, whom his master has set over his household, to give them their food at the proper time? 46 Blessed is that servant whom his master when he comes will find so doing. 47 Truly, I say to you, he will set him over all his possessions. 48 But if that wicked servant says to himself, 'My master is delayed,' 49 and begins to beat his fellow servants, and eats and drinks with the drunken, 50 the master of that servant will come on a day when he does not expect him and at an hour he does not know, 51 and will punish him, and put him with the hypocrites; there men will weep and gnash their teeth.

Luke makes all of these predictions personal saying, "Take heed of your self." (Ref. Parable of the Ten Maidens, Matt. 25:6ff.)

Remain faithful

Matthew 24:45-51

Comment
Matthew defines the faithful servant as the one who is found waiting and prepared. Likewise the unfaithful servant is the one who has not prepared and thinks he has freedom and license to do as he pleases.

Jesus spoke in parables

Matthew 25:1-13
1 "Then the kingdom of heaven shall be compared to ten maidens who took their lamps and went to meet the bridegroom. 2 Five of them were foolish, and five were wise. 3 For when the foolish took their lamps, they took no oil with them; 4 but the wise took flasks of oil with their lamps. 5 As the bridegroom was delayed, they all slumbered and slept. 6 But at midnight there was a cry, 'Behold, the bridegroom! Come out to meet him.' 7 Then all those maidens rose and trimmed their lamps. 8 And the foolish said to the wise, 'Give us some of your oil, for our lamps are going out. 9 But the wise replied, 'Perhaps there will not be enough for us and for you; go rather to the dealers and buy for yourselves.' 10 And while they went to buy, the bridegroom came, and those who were ready went in with him to the marriage feast; and the door was shut. 11 Afterward the other maidens came also, saying, 'Lord, lord, open to us.' 12 But he replied, 'Truly, I say to you, I do not know you.' 13 Watch therefore, for you know neither the day nor the hour.

Jesus spoke in parables

Matthew 25:1-13

All of chapter 25 is unique to Matthew.

Comment

The setting for this parable is a Palestinian wedding. The bridal party waits at the home of the groom. The guest will also be found there. The bridesmaid's responsibility was to escort the groom to meet the bride when he arrives.

Five of the maidens are called foolish, because they brought no extra oil with them. They assumed that the bridegroom would be there without delay. Therefore they made no preparation for the unexpected.

Five of the maidens were called wise because they did bring extra oil. They were ready for any eventuality.

At midnight the bridegroom arrived. Having left their lamps burning the ten maidens all trimmed their wicks. The five foolish maidens were now in a distressed position. They did not have spare oil to replenish their supply. They ask the wise maidens to share their reserve supply of oil. The wise maidens

	responded gently but firmly that to give them of their reserve supply would mean all would have less than they needed for the procession. They gently suggested these girls go to the dealer to buy more oil. The lesson is clear, Jesus said, be prepared because you do not know what the future holds.

No explanation for the bridegroom's delay

We are given no explanation for the bridegroom's delay. Realizing the bridegroom would be delayed, the ten maidens laid down to rest until he arrived.

It would be quite unlikely that the dealer would awaken and sell to them.

At some point later, the five unwise maidens made their way and banged on the closed door. They were told they could not come in and in fact the statement was, "I do not know you."

The Talents	*The Talents*
Matthew 25:14-30 14 "For it will be as when a man going on a journey called his servants and entrusted to them his property; 15 to one he gave five talents, to another two, to another one, to each according to his ability. Then he went away. 16 He who had received the five talents went at once and	**Matthew 25:14-30** **Comment** This parable is a continuation of the discussion of "What is the kingdom of heaven like?" Jesus said, "A man was going to go on a journey, he divided his business among three of

traded with them; and he made five talents more. [17] So also, he who had the two talents made two talents more. [18] But he who had received the one talent went and dug in the ground and hid his master's money. [19] Now after a long time the master of those servants came and settled accounts with them. [20] And he who had received the five talents came forward, bringing five talents more, saying, 'Master, you delivered to me five talents; here I have made five talents more.' [21] His master said to him, 'Well done, good and faithful servant; you have been faithful over a little, I will set you over much; enter into the joy of your master.' [22] And he also who had the two talents came forward, saying, 'Master, you delivered to me two talents; here I have made two talents more.' [23] His master said to him, 'Well done, good and faithful servant; you have been faithful over a little, I will set you over much; enter into the joy of your master.' [24] He also who had received the one talent came forward, saying, 'Master, I knew you to be a hard man, reaping where you did not sow, and gathering where you did not winnow; [25] so I was afraid, and I went and hid your talent in the ground. Here you have what is yours.' [26] But his master answered him, 'You wicked and

his servants, the first servant received five talents, the second received three talents, and the final servant received one talent. It is significant that each received talents commensurate with his abilities.

After a long time the man returned home. Each servant then gave an accounting of his stewardship. The steward with five talents has made five more. The steward with three had made three more. Both of these received a commendation from the man, 'Well done good faithful servant.' The third servant had made no profit on what the man had entrusted to him. The best he could do was to return what the man had given him in the beginning, one talent.

The man who received the one talent is depicted as being of a mean spirit. He excuses his negligence by blaming the man. He accuses him of thievery and dishonesty."

The lessons here are clear. We will not be judged by comparison to others. We will stand or fall on our own individual merit.

slothful servant! You knew that I reap where I have not sowed, and gather where I have not winnowed? 27 Then you ought to have invested my money with the bankers, and at my coming I should have received what was my own with interest. 28 So take the talent from him, and give it to him who has the ten talents. 29 For to every one who has will more be given, and he will have abundance; but from him who has not, even what he has will be taken away. 30 And cast the worthless servant into the outer darkness; there men will weep and gnash their teeth.'

Remain vigilant

Luke 12:35-48
35 "Let your loins be girded and your lamps burning, 36 and be like men who are waiting for their master to come home from the marriage feast, so that they may open to him at once when he comes and knocks. 37 Blessed are those servants whom the master finds awake when he comes; truly, I say to you, he will gird himself and have them sit at table, and he will come and serve them. 38 If he comes in the second watch, or in the third, and finds them so, blessed are those servants! 39 But know this, that if the householder had known at what hour the thief was coming,

Remain vigilant

Luke 12:35-48

Comment

Rather than maidens Luke speaks of men servants. They are told to put on their clothes and light their lamps. They are charged to remain alert as they waited for their master's return from the wedding. Their valiance would allow them to open the door even before he knocks. The master would be so pleased that he would invite them to sit at table with him. If he served them their joy would abound.

he would not have left his house to be broken into. 40 You also must be ready; for the Son of man is coming at an unexpected hour." 41 Peter said, "Lord, are you telling this parable for us or for all?" 42 And the Lord said, "Who then is the faithful and wise steward, whom his master will set over his household, to give them their portion of food at the proper time? 43 Blessed is that servant whom his master when he comes will find so doing. 44 Truly, I say to you, he will set him over all his possessions. 45 But if that servant says to himself, 'My master is delayed in coming,' and begins to beat the menservants and the maidservants, and to eat and drink and get drunk, 46 the master of that servant will come on a day when he does not expect him and at an hour he does not know, and will punish him, and put him with the unfaithful. 47 And that servant who knew his master's will, but did not make ready or act according to his will, shall receive a severe beating. 48 But he who did not know, and did what deserved a beating, shall receive a light beating. Every one to whom much is given, of him will much be required; and of him to whom men commit much they will demand the more.

Jesus spoke another truism. If a householder knew his house was in danger of being broken into by burglars he would prepare to defend it. Jesus said, you also must be ready, because you do not know what hour the Son will return. Peter began to get the point that this parable was aimed at the Inner-Circle. Jesus said the servant that is doing the will of the master is the servant the master will reward. The servant who takes liberties with the responsibilities the master entrusted to him will find himself severely reprimanded. One who does not know what is expected and still makes mistakes will be only lightly punished.

Luke closes with a powerful statement to all who enjoy plenty, "Every one to whom much is given, of him will much be required; and of him to whom men commit much they will demand the more." One's blessings are not their exclusive possession.

This parable recorded in Luke
Contains a strong resemblance to Matthew

This parable recorded in Luke bears strong resemblance to what we have just read in Matthew. There are several significant differences that we shall point out.

This statement is the exact opposite of what was really expected to happen. "I say to you, he will gird himself and have them sit at table and he will come and serve them."

The servants were always expected to be ready and waiting. The master would never dream of serving them at his own table. Therefore, we conclude this parable was Jesus' way of saying how different things will be in the kingdom of God.

When Jesus returns	*When Jesus returns*
Matthew 25:31-46	**Matthew 25:31-46**
31 "When the Son of man comes in his glory, and all the angels with him, then he will sit on his glorious throne. 32 Before him will be gathered all the nations, and he will separate them one from another as a shepherd separates the sheep from the goats, 33 and he will place the sheep at his right hand, but the goats at the left. 34 Then the King will say to those at his right hand, 'Come, O blessed of my Father, inherit the kingdom prepared for you from the foundation of the world; 35 for I was hungry and you gave me food, I was thirsty and you gave me drink, I was a stranger and you welcomed me, 36 I was naked and you clothed me, I was sick and you visited me, I was in prison and you came to	**Comment**
	The culmination of these predictions would be when Jesus returned. Then he will sit upon his throne to act as judge. All humanity will come before him, and he will separate them as a shepherd separates sheep from goats.
	One should not miss the comparison of sheep, the Good Shepherd, and the flock of the Lord. The sheep are those who have shown the same compassion, love, and concern that Jesus showed.
	Almost every human being sooner or later during their lifetime comes into contact with

me.' 37 Then the righteous will answer him, 'Lord, when did we see thee hungry and feed thee, or thirsty and give thee drink? 38 And when did we see thee a stranger and welcome thee, or naked and clothe thee? 39 And when did we see thee sick or in prison and visit thee?' 40 And the King will answer them, 'Truly, I say to you, as you did it to one of the least of these my brethren, you did it to me.' 41 Then he will say to those at his left hand, 'Depart from me, you cursed, into the eternal fire prepared for the devil and his angels; 42 for I was hungry and you gave me no food, I was thirsty and you gave me no drink, 43 I was a stranger and you did not welcome me, naked and you did not clothe me, sick and in prison and you did not visit me.' 44 Then they also will answer, 'Lord, when did we see thee hungry or thirsty or a stranger or naked or sick or in prison, and did not minister to thee?' 45 Then he will answer them, 'Truly, I say to you, as you did it not to one of the least of these, you did it not to me.' 46 And they will go away into eternal punishment, but the righteous into eternal life."

someone who is hungry, or one who is thirsty, or is a stranger to them, or one who has need of better clothing, or one who is sick, or one who is behind prison bars.

The difference between those who go into the kingdom of God and those who go into the eternal disappointment is how they have responded to these persons who crossed their path during their lifetime.

Chapter 6

Holy Week: Wednesday Evening - The Last Supper

THE UPPER ROOM

There is rarely a comparable report in the Synoptic Gospels, (Mark, Matthew, and Luke), corresponding to John's account.

Wednesday evening, The Last Supper Mark 14:17; Matthew 26:20; Luke 22:14	*Wednesday evening, The Last Supper* Mark 14:17; Matthew 26:20; Luke 22:14
Mark 14:17 And when it was evening he came with the twelve. **Matthew 26:20** When it was evening, he sat at table with the twelve disciples; **Luke 22:14** And when the hour came, he sat at table, and the apostles with him.	**Comment** Returning from the Mount of Olives Jesus lead the Inner-Circle to an upper room that had been placed at their disposal. Those who prepared the meal were already there. Jesus and the remainder of the disciples joined them. As they stood together making conversation, no one made an attempt to perform the act of hospitality.
Jesus' hour had come! **John 13:1** Now before the feast of the Passover, when Jesus knew that his hour had come to depart out of this world to the Father,	*Jesus' hour had come!* **John 13:1** **Comment** The long awaited hour had now come. Only Jesus understood

having loved his own who were in the world, he loved them to the end.

that God had chosen this to be Jesus' hour. From the beginning Jesus had loved the members of the Inner-Circle, and he would love them to the end.

Judas Iscariot, Simon's son, will betray Jesus

John 13:2
And during supper, when the devil had already put it into the heart of Judas Iscariot, Simon's son, to betray him,

Judas Iscariot, Simon's son, will betray Jesus

John 13:2

Comment
The one who will betray Jesus is exposed by name, Judas Iscariot.

God's time had come; Jesus' hour had started to tick. What God has set in motion cannot be stopped.

John in v. 2 says *diabolos*, (devil) which means false accuser, slanderer, a man who, by opposing the cause of God, may be said to act the part of the devil or to side with him.

Jesus prepares to wash their feet

John 13:3-11
3 Jesus, knowing that the Father had given all things into his hands, and that he had come from God and was going to God, 4 rose from supper, laid aside his garments, and girded himself with a towel. 5 Then he poured

Jesus prepares to wash their feet

John 13:3-11

Comment
When Jesus knelt before Peter to wash his feet, Peter adamantly refused to allow it. When Peter understood what it meant he went overboard, asking that his

water into a basin, and began to wash the disciples' feet, and to wipe them with the towel with which he was girded. 6 He came to Simon Peter; and Peter said to him, "Lord, do you wash my feet?" 7 Jesus answered him, "What I am doing you do not know now, but afterward you will understand." 8 Peter said to him, "You shall never wash my feet." Jesus answered him, "If I do not wash you, you have no part in me." 9 Simon Peter said to him, "Lord, not my feet only but also my hands and my head!" 10 Jesus said to him, "He who has bathed does not need to wash, except for his feet, but he is clean all over; and you are clean, but not every one of you." 11 For he knew who was to betray him; that was why he said, "You are not all clean."

entire person be washed. Jesus wanted all of his disciples to understand the attitude of one's heart, not the physical act that follows is what counts.

What have I done?

John 13:12-16
12 When he had washed their feet, and taken his garments, and resumed his place, he said to them, "Do you know what I have done to you? 13 You call me Teacher and Lord; and you are right, for so I am. 14 If I then, your Lord and Teacher, have washed your feet, you also ought to wash one another's feet.

What have I done?

John 13:12-16

Comment
Pride kept getting in the way of the disciples' willingness to serve one another. Jesus reminded them that they referred to him as Teacher and Lord and this was justly so. He also pointed out the student is never greater than the teacher. He

15 For I have given you an example, that you also should do as I have done to you. 16 Truly, truly, I say to you, a servant is not greater than his master; nor is he who is sent greater than he who sent him.

was making the point that they were to follow his example in humility.

I am telling you before hand

John 13:17-19

17 If you know these things, blessed are you if you do them. 18 I am not speaking of you all; I know whom I have chosen; it is that the scripture may be fulfilled, 'He who ate my bread has lifted his heel against me.' 19 I tell you this now, before it takes place, that when it does take place you may believe that I am he.

I am telling you before hand

John 13:17-19

Comment

Understanding what Jesus was talking about was not sufficient. Doing it was what really mattered. Jesus began the process of revealing his betrayer. He quoted Psalms 41:9 to set the stage. The Greek definition of the word "lifted" is, "to be lifted up with pride, to exalt one's self." The Greek definition of the word "heel" is, "to injure one by trickery" (figure borrowed either from kicking or from a wrestler tripping up his antagonist).

By saying this Jesus revealed what was about to take place.

Whoever receives the Disciple Receives Jesus and the Father

**John 13:20;
Matthew 10:40-42;
Luke 10:16**

Whoever receives the Disciple Receives Jesus and the Father

**John 13:20;
Matthew 10:40-42;
Luke 10:16**

John 13:20 20 Truly, truly, I say to you, he who receives any one whom I send receives me; and he who receives me receives him who sent me."	**Comment** When one receives the disciples they are also receiving Jesus and the Father. Some would receive them as they would a prophet. Others would receive them as righteous men.
Matthew 10:40-42 40 "He who receives you receives me, and he who receives me receives him who sent me. 41 He who receives a prophet because he is a prophet shall receive a prophet's reward, and he who receives a righteous man because he is a righteous man shall receive a righteous man's reward. 42 And whoever gives to one of these little ones even a cup of cold water because he is a disciple, truly, I say to you, he shall not lose his reward."	The rewards God bestowed or will bestow are for good deeds and positive efforts by others. Matthew and Luke offer nearly the same thought.
Luke 10:16 "He who hears you hears me, and he who rejects you rejects me, and he who rejects me rejects him who sent me."	

One of you will betray me

Mark 14:18-21;
Matthew 26:21-25;
Luke 22:14-16; 21-23;
John 13:21

One of you will betray me

Mark 14:18-21;
Matthew 26:21-25;
Luke 22:14-16; 21-23;
John 13:21

Mark 14:18-21 18 And as they were at table eating, Jesus said, "Truly, I say to you, one of you will betray me, one who is eating with me."	**Comment** Mark gives us the basic report echoed by the other evangelist. Only Matthew records Judas asking, "Is it I?" Jesus

19 They began to be sorrowful, and to say to him one after another, "Is it I?" 20 He said to them, "It is one of the twelve, one who is dipping bread into the dish with me. 21 For the Son of man goes as it is written of him, but woe to that man by whom the Son of man is betrayed! It would have been better for that man if he had not been born."

Matthew 26:21-25
21 and as they were eating, he said, "Truly, I say to you, one of you will betray me." 22 And they were very sorrowful, and began to say to him one after another, "Is it I, Lord?" 23 He answered, "He who has dipped his hand in the dish with me, will betray me. 24 The Son of man goes as it is written of him, but woe to that man by whom the Son of man is betrayed! It would have been better for that man if he had not been born." 25 Judas, who betrayed him, said, "Is it I, Master?" He said to him, "You have said so."

Luke 22:15-16; 21-23
15 And he said to them, "I have earnestly desired to eat this passover with you before I suffer; 16 for I tell you I shall not eat it until it is fulfilled in the kingdom of God." 21 But behold the hand of him who betrays me is with me on the table. 22 For the Son of man goes as it has

responded, "You have said so."Luke unmistakably identifies the presence of Satan at the last supper. This is clearly seen in the exchange between Jesus and Judas.

been determined; but woe to that man by whom he is betrayed!"
23 And they began to question one another, which of them it was that would do this.

John 13:21
21 When Jesus had thus spoken, he was troubled in spirit, and testified, "Truly, truly, I say to you, one of you will betray me."

Biblical References

Mark and Matthew, refer to Isaiah 53:1-12.
1 Who has believed what we have heard? And to whom has the arm of the LORD been revealed? 2 For he grew up before him like a young plant, and like a root out of dry ground; he had no form or comeliness that we should look at him, and no beauty that we should desire him. 3 He was despised and rejected by men; a man of sorrows, and acquainted with grief; and as one from whom men hide their faces he was despised, and we esteemed him not.

4 Surely he has borne our grief's and carried our sorrows; yet we esteemed him stricken, smitten by God, and afflicted. 5 But he was wounded for our transgressions, he was bruised for our iniquities; upon him was the chastisement that made us whole, and with his stripes we are healed. 6 All we like sheep have gone astray; we have turned every one to his own way; and the LORD has laid on him the iniquity of us all. 7 He was oppressed, and he was afflicted, yet he opened not his mouth; like a lamb that is led to the slaughter, and like a sheep that before its shearers is dumb, so he opened not his mouth. 8 By oppression and judgment he was taken away; and as for his generation, who considered that he was cut off out of the land of the living, stricken for the transgression of my people?

9 And they made his grave with the wicked and with a rich man in his death, although he had done no violence, and there was no deceit in his mouth. 10 Yet it was the will of the LORD to bruise him; he has put him to grief; when he makes himself an offering for sin, he shall see his offspring, he shall prolong his days; the will of the LORD shall prosper in his hand; 11 he shall see the fruit of the travail of his soul and be satisfied; by his knowledge shall the righteous one, my servant, make many to be accounted righteous; and he shall bear their iniquities. 12 Therefore I will divide him a portion with the great, and he shall divide the spoil with the strong; because he poured out his soul to death, and was numbered with the transgressors; yet he bore the sin of many, and made intercession for the transgressors.

Lord who will betray you?

John 13:22-29
22 The disciples looked at one another, uncertain of whom he spoke. 23 One of his disciples, whom Jesus loved, was lying close to the breast of Jesus; 24 so Simon Peter beckoned to him and said, "Tell us who it is of whom he speaks." 25 So lying thus, close to the breast of Jesus, he said to him, "Lord, who is it?" 26 Jesus answered, "It is he to whom I shall give this morsel when I have dipped it." So when he had dipped the morsel, he gave it to Judas, the son of Simon Iscariot. 27 Then after the morsel, Satan entered into him. Jesus said to him, "What you are going to do, do quickly." 28 Now no one at the table knew why he said this to him. 29 Some thought that, because Judas had the money box, Jesus was telling him, "Buy what we need for the feast"; or, that he should give something to the poor.

Lord who will betray you?

John13:22-29

Comment
Only John gives us this body of information. The Inner-Circle was shocked by Jesus' words that he would be betrayed.

John also provides a clue as to the seating arrangement at the meal as he describes it in verses 23-25. All of the diners would have been in a reclining position heads toward the center; feet toward the outer circle.

In v. 27 John uses the word *Satanas* (Satan) which means, "The prince of evil spirits, the inveterate adversary of God and Christ, who entices apostasy from God and to sin circumventing men by his wiles."

Triclinium

The best statement of the seating arrangement I have come across is this by Dr. James Fleming. "A 'triclinium' is a three-sided horseshoe-shaped table which was the common seating arrangement for a meal by wealthy persons in the Roman period. Jews believed that for one night a year, at least, they ought to eat reclining to show that they were wealthy in spirit, if not in material goods. Slaves ate standing; free persons ate reclining."

The left-hand table was the most important table and the host normally had a right hand man and a left hand man on either side of him. If the friend who offered the room had been at the feast, he certainly would have volunteered to wash the disciples' feet (Luke 22:11). Jesus was the host.

When reclining at a meal it was the custom to rest on one's left elbow and to eat with the right hand. John 13:23 says that JOHN was leaning on Jesus' chest. This requires him to be in the right hand position. One might have expected Jesus to have offered this place to Peter, or James, or John as they were the closest circle of his friends (Luke 9:28; Mark 14:33).

There are two indications that JUDAS was reclining at the left hand of Jesus: (1.) there was the custom of offering a piece of meat ("the sop") to the guest of honor (John 13:26), who was seated close enough to Jesus to be eating from the same dishes because when John inquired of Jesus who would betray him, Jesus answered, "Someone dipping in the same bowl with me." It seems that Jesus was trying to give every opportunity to Judas, even giving him the place of honor at the Last Supper! Judas was having trouble with Jesus' understanding of the role of the Messiah. If this reconstruction is correct, another implication is that Judas had the Lord leaning on his chest throughout the meal. This must have heightened the conflict going on within his heart as he had already arranged to turn Jesus over to the authorities (Matt. 26:14-16, John 14:31-38).

There are three indications that PETER was reclining in the very last seat of all. All of these evidences are indirect however. (1) Luke records that there was a dispute over who was greatest as they walked into the guest chamber (Luke 22:24). This rivalry evidently being rather common (Mark 9:34). Because Jesus put Peter in charge of preparing the lamb sacrifice (if the meal was a Passover Seder) and making the arrangements (read Luke 22:8), they both probably pictured themselves sitting on either side of the host, Jesus. It may be that in reaction to Jesus inviting Judas to have the seat of the guest of honor that the imperious and impulsive Peter in an "I'll show you" attitude, stomped over to the very last and least seat, which was at the opposite corner of the table. (2) The account of Jesus washing the disciples' feet seems to imply that Peter was about the last to have his feet washed (John 13:6). This would be expected if the reconstruction suggested above is correct. Actually, the person reclining in the least seat should have volunteered to do the foot washing! (3) Peter had to be in a position where he could get John's attention and motion for him to ask of Jesus who the betrayer would be, without feeling that Jesus or the others would necessarily overhear him (John 13:23-26).

One must be cautious in specifying that the seating had to be as pictured above, but in light of it being a reclining meal at a "furnished" room, this reconstruction seems to be a reasonable, educated guess.

Judas departs	*Judas departs*
John 13:30	**John 13:30**
So, after receiving the morsel, he [Judas] immediately went out; and it was night.	**Comment** Judas made his exit before Jesus instituted the Eucharist or Holy Communion. Thus Judas did not receive what we know as the Holy Communion or the forgiveness it proclaimed (Matt. 26:28).
The Bread and the Cup	*The Bread and the Cup*
Mark 14:22-25; Matthew 26:26-29; Luke 22:17-20	**Mark 14:22-25; Matthew 26:26-29; Luke 22:17-20**
Mark 14:22-25 22 And as they were eating, he took bread, and blessed, and	**Comment** Mark, Matthew, and Luke render almost the same

broke it, and gave it to them, and said, "Take; this is my body." 23 And he took a cup, and when he had given thanks he gave it to them, and they all drank of it. 24 And he said to them, "This is my blood of the covenant, which is poured out for many. 25 Truly, I say to you, I shall not drink again of the fruit of the vine until that day when I drink it new in the kingdom of God."

Matthew 26:26-29
26 Now as they were eating, Jesus took bread, and blessed, and broke it, and gave it to the disciples and said, "Take, eat; this is my body." 27 And he took a cup, and when he had given thanks he gave it to them, saying, "Drink of it, all of you; 28 for this is my blood of the covenant, which is poured out for many for the forgiveness of sins. 29 I tell you I shall not drink again of this fruit of the vine until that day when I drink it new with you in my Father's kingdom."

Luke 22:17-20
17 And he took a cup, and when he had given thanks he said, "Take this, and divide it among yourselves; 18 for I tell you that from now on I shall not drink of the fruit of the vine until the kingdom of God comes." 19 And he took bread, and when he had given thanks he broke it and

account. Mark and Matthew sequence the elements bread first followed by the cup. Luke reverses the sequence stating the cup first and then the bread. Matthew states, the sacrifice is for the forgiveness of sin. Luke adds "do this in remembrance of me," which is unique to his account.

Christian believers today may not receive the same impact these words had upon the Inner-Circle. Being literal minded individuals, the Inner-Circle would have been repulsed by the idea of eating Jesus' flesh and drinking his blood. Using figurative language had caused many of Jesus' followers great consternation, the Pharisees had been repulsed at the idea Jesus was the breath of life, the hearers at Capernaum deserted because of the "I am" statements. It should be recognized that by the time the evangelists wrote their accounts, the sacrament of Holy Communion had been well defined and established within the Christian community.

gave it to them, saying, "This is my body which is given for you. Do this in remembrance of me." 20 And likewise the cup after supper, saying, "This cup which is poured out for you is the new covenant in my blood.

Table talk turns into a dispute

Luke 22:24-30
24 A dispute also arose among them, which of them was to be regarded as the greatest. 25 And he said to them, "The kings of the Gentiles exercise lordship over them; and those in authority over them are called benefactors. 26 But not so with you; rather let the greatest among you become as the youngest, and the leader as one who serves. 27 For which is the greater, one who sits at table, or one who serves? Is it not the one who sits at table? But I am among you as one who serves. 28 "You are those who have continued with me in my trials; 29 and I assign to you, as my Father assigned to me, a kingdom, 30 that you may eat and drink at my table in my kingdom, and sit on thrones judging the twelve tribes of Israel.

Table talk turns into a dispute

Luke 22:24-30

Comment
This is Jesus' last gathering with his colleagues. He told them he was giving them a special place in his reign.

Luke places the dispute about who would have preeminence within the context of the celebration of the Last Supper. Mark places the conflict before their entry into Jerusalem. Such disputes over power and prestige had no place in Jesus' Kingdom.

Luke exposes Satan's explicit role of creating division and chaos among the Inner-Circle. It is a reminder to the reader of the critical need for not compromising one's commitment to Jesus and by doing so becomes a victory for God's avowed enemy.

What does it mean to be, "Glorified?"

John 13:31-35

31 When he had gone out, Jesus said, "Now is the Son of man glorified, and in him God is glorified; 32 if God is glorified in him, God will also glorify him in himself, and glorify him at once. 33 Little children, yet a little while I am with you. You will seek me; and as I said to the Jews so now I say to you, 'Where I am going you cannot come.' 34 A new commandment I give to you, that you love one another; even as I have loved you, that you also love one another. 35 By this all men will know that you are my disciples, if you have love for one another."

What does it mean to be, "Glorified?"

John 13:31-35

Comment

It is not by Jesus' death that he will be glorified, but rather by his resurrection. Through the resurrection, Jesus will be honored and respected and recognized as the Son of God. God the Father will be recognized by His mighty act in His Son. Calling the Inner-Circle "Little children" is a high compliment when we remember the esteem Jesus held for children.

Jesus reiterated to the larger crowd that where he was going the crowd could not follow. Neither could the Inner-Circle.

This was an awesome statement. While other leaders sought to be remembered for their prowess Jesus wanted his followers to be recognized because of their love for each other. By the act of loving and being loved the world would recognize them as his followers.

Peter and the Crowing Rooster

John 13:36-38

36 Simon Peter said to him, "Lord, where are you going?" Jesus answered, "Where I am going you cannot follow me now; but you shall follow afterward." 37 Peter said to him, "Lord, why cannot I follow you now? I will lay down my life for you." 38 Jesus answered, "Will you lay down your life for me? Truly, truly, I say to you, the cock will not crow, till you have denied me three times.

Simon, Satan demanded you

Luke 22:31-38

31 "Simon, Simon, behold, Satan demanded to have you, that he might sift you like wheat, 32 but I have prayed for you that your faith may not fail; and when you have turned again, strengthen your brethren." 33 And he said to him, "Lord, I am ready to go with you to prison and to death." 34 He said, "I tell you, Peter, the cock will not crow this day, until you three times deny that you know me." 35 And he said to them, "When I sent you out with no purse or bag or sandals, did you lack anything?" They said, "Nothing." 36 He said to them, "But now, let him who has a purse take it, and

Peter and the Crowing Rooster

John 13:36-38

Comment

Peter wanted to know where Jesus was going that he could not go with him. Jesus gave some clarification saying, "Not now but later you will follow me." Peter then boldly stated his willingness to die for Jesus. Jesus' reply both stunned and humiliated Peter. Peter could not help but wonder what Jesus meant by the crowing cock.

Simon, Satan demanded you

Comment

Luke 22:31-38

This is Luke's version.

What a fearsome thought! Satan demanded to have Peter under his control. Satan wanted to do more to Peter than he had done to Job. Jesus prayed that Peter's faith would not fail him. Jesus' statement reveals that obviously it would fail him at least temporarily. But when he had regained it he was to strengthen his brothers.

Peter would not let the matter rest. He reaffirmed his statement

likewise a bag. And let him who has no sword sell his mantle and buy one. 37 For I tell you that this scripture must be fulfilled in me, 'And he was reckoned with transgressors'; for what is written about me has its fulfilment." 38 And they said, "Look, Lord, here are two swords." And he said to them, "It is enough."

that he was willing to go to prison or death with Jesus. Jesus makes it crystal clear the cock would not crow before Peter had denied him three times. This reprimand must have reminded Peter of his humiliation when Jesus said, "you are like a Satan to me."

The Inner-Circle remembered vividly their successes in the name of Jesus when he sent them out two by two. On this occasion however, Jesus gave them entirely different marching orders. Any who was not armed should sell his mantle and buy arms for the evening.

Luke includes this uncharacteristic story of Jesus urging his disciples to acquire swords for the confrontation with the authorities that soon will occur. Two swords will be enough for this evening's work.

Luke quotes the prophet Isaiah

Therefore I will divide him a portion with the great, and he shall divide the spoil with the strong; because he poured out his soul to death, and was numbered with the transgressors; yet he bore the sin of many, and made intercession for the transgressors. – Isaiah 53:12

John says Jesus delivered his Farewell address at this time

The following passage is referred to as Jesus' Farewell Address to his Inner-Circle. The farewell address has a long history in the Bible. To cite a few: Jacob's is found in Genesis chapter 49, Joshua's is found in Joshua chapters 23 and 24, Moses' address takes up much of the book of Deuteronomy, David's is found in 1 Chronicles chapters 28 and 29, and Paul's final address can be found in Acts 20:17–38.

Typically these addresses contain a gathering of the followers or family; an announcement of the imminent departure or death; a review of the person's life; names a successor, prophecies, promises, blessings; final instructions; and prayer.

	Jesus' Farewell Address
	Comment
	The farewell address follows the following format:
	The gathering of followers; v.1.
	The announcement of imminent departure or death; vv. 2-8.
	The review of the person's life; vv. 9-15.
	Names a successor; v. 16.
	Gives a prophecy; v. 17-24.
	Gives a promise; vv. 25-26.
	Pronounces a blessing; vv. 27-28.
	Final instructions; vv. 29-31.
Let your hearts not be troubled	*Let your hearts not be troubled*
John 14:1-7	**John 14:1-7**

1 "Let not your hearts be troubled; believe in God, believe also in me. 2 In my Father's house are many rooms; if it were not so, would I have told you that I go to prepare a place for you? 3 And when I go and prepare a place for you, I will come again and will take you to myself, that where I am you may be also. 4 And you know the way where I am going." 5 Thomas said to him, "Lord, we do not know where you are going; how can we know the way?" 6 Jesus said to him, "I am the way, and the truth, and the life; no one comes to the Father, but by me. 7 If you had known me, you would have known my Father also; henceforth you know him and have seen him."	**Comment** These words were spoken in conjunction with the Last Supper in the Upper Room. The atmosphere had become very heavy after the announcement that one of them would betray Jesus. The Inner-Circle fully understood the concept of this statement of many rooms. The custom of the time was at the marriage of a son the father would build another room on the home. Large families would have a house with many rooms. Jesus reassured the disciples not to be troubled saying he will come later, and they know the way to the place he is going. Jesus believed he had already prepared them to be able to fully understand what he meant. Surely they would understand his time on earth was coming to a close and he would soon be back in the realm of his Father in Heaven. Thomas said Lord we do not know where you are going how in the world can we know the way?

Some think of Thomas as a doubter

Some think of Thomas as a doubter. I think of Thomas as a pragmatist. He could see the bottom line and did not waste time asking the critical questions. In essence Thomas said, "Why are you getting ready to leave us? Judas is not here, where are you planning to go?" Jesus responded that he was the way to truth and life, and then moved the dialogue in a new direction.

Lord, show us the Father

John 14:8-11

8 Philip said to him, "Lord, show us the Father, and we shall be satisfied." 9 Jesus said to him, "Have I been with you so long, and yet you do not know me, Philip? He who has seen me has seen the Father; how can you say, 'Show us the Father'? 10 Do you not believe that I am in the Father and the Father in me? The words that I say to you I do not speak on my own authority; but the Father who dwells in me does his works. 11 Believe me that I am in the Father and the Father in me; or else believe me for the sake of the works themselves.

Lord, show us the Father

John 14:8-11

Comment

To paraphrase Jesus, "Have I failed so miserably? Have I been with you all this time and failed to help you see the Father in me? Have you experienced all that we have done and failed to see the hand of the Father working and guiding me?" What a sense of failure Jesus experienced by the questions of two of his Inner-Circle; Thomas and Philip.

Whatever you ask in my name

John 14:12-14

12 "Truly, truly, I say to you, he who believes in me will also do the works that I do; and greater works than these will he do, because I go to the Father. 13 Whatever you ask in my name, I will do it, that the Father may be glorified in the Son; 14 if you ask anything in my name, I will do it.

Whatever you ask in my name

John 14:12-14

Comment

Believing in Jesus would in part be manifested in doing the works that Jesus had done. He then cast a vision that his followers would do greater things than he had done. This was because Jesus was going to the Father. To ask in the name of Jesus was to ask in accord with the spirit of Jesus. In those cases, Jesus would grant the request.

If you love me, you will keep my commandments	***If you love me, you will keep my commandments***
John 14:15-17 15 "If you love me, you will keep my commandments. 16 And I will pray the Father, and he will give you another Counselor, to be with you for ever, 17 even the Spirit of truth, whom the world cannot receive, because it neither sees him nor knows him; you know him, for he dwells with you, and will be in you.	**John 14:15-17** **Comment** The Holy Spirit would soon be on the scene. The world (non-believers) could not receive the Holy Spirit. Jesus promised to send the Holy Spirit to the disciples to teach them the truths they were not yet prepared to hear.

What are Jesus' commandments?

"This is my commandment, that you love one another as I have loved you. – John 15:12

The second is this, 'You shall love your neighbor as yourself.' There is no other commandment greater than these." – Mark 12:31

Because I live, you will live also

John 14:18-20

18 "I will not leave you desolate; I will come to you. 19 Yet a little while, and the world will see me no more, but you will see me; because I live, you will live also. 20 In that day you will know that I am in my Father, and you in me, and I in you.

He who does not love me does not keep my words

John 14:21-24

21 He who has my commandments and keeps them, he it is who loves me; and he who loves me will be loved by my Father, and I will love him and manifest myself to him." 22 Judas (not Iscariot) said to him, "Lord, how is it that you will manifest yourself to us, and not to the world?" 23 Jesus answered him, "If a man loves me, he will keep my word, and my Father will love him, and we will come to him and make our home with him. 24 He who does not love me does not keep my words; and the word which you hear is not mine but the Father's who sent me.

Because I live, you will live also

John 14:18-20

Comment

The reign of the Kingdom of Heaven unites believers with the Father by uniting them with Jesus who said, "I am in the father and you are in me and I am in you."

He who does not love me does not keep my words

John 14:21-24

Comment

Jesus said keeping his commandments constituted an act of love by his followers. This leads to the realization that the Father also loves them.

Judas asked how could Jesus reveal himself to them and not to the world? He answered the Father and I will come and make our home within those who love us. We are not welcome in the heart of the unbeliever.

These things I have spoken while I am still with you

John 14:25-31

25 "These things I have spoken to you, while I am still with you. 26 But the Counselor, the Holy Spirit, whom the Father will send in my name, he will teach you all things, and bring to your remembrance all that I have said to you. 27 Peace I leave with you; my peace I give to you; not as the world gives do I give to you. Let not your hearts be troubled, neither let them be afraid. 28 You heard me say to you, 'I go away, and I will come to you.' If you loved me, you would have rejoiced, because I go to the Father; for the Father is greater than I. 29 And now I have told you before it takes place, so that when it does take place, you may believe. 30 I will no longer talk much with you, for the ruler of this world is coming. He has no power over me; 31 but I do as the Father has commanded me, so that the world may know that I love the Father. Rise, let us go hence.

These things I have spoken while I am still with you

John 14:25-31

Comment

Jesus did not expect his disciples to remember everything he had told them. When the Father bestowed the Holy Spirit upon them he would enable them to remember everything.

The peace of which Jesus speaks is spiritual peace. It is the confidence that no matter how chaotic the world may be this peace resides in the knowledge and presence of Jesus in the believer. Therefore there was no reason to be afraid of the future.

Jesus' statement in verse 28 opens our understanding to the heart break the death of a loved one brings. Even when one knows that the deceased was presently in the hands of God there is the sadness of physical loss. Time was running out, Jesus knew the end was coming quickly. He wanted them to hear everything from his own lips before it happened.

The next words Jesus utters are some of the most powerful in the entire Gospel. Jesus' reference to the ruler of this world means nothing other than the Devil. The Devil has no control over Jesus. He will carry out his dastardly deed only because it is permitted by God.

Jesus then arose and said, "Let us be going." Jesus continued to teach as they walked out of Jerusalem, and up the Mount of olives.

I am the true vine

John 15:1-11

Comment

Jesus used the metaphor of the grapevine. He speaks of himself as the vine, and God as the vine dresser.

Bearing and not bearing fruit is a major theme of Jesus' teaching ministry. He expects without exception, that his followers spread his word everywhere. Those that bear no fruit will be cut off and thrown into the fire. The branches that bear fruit will be pruned so that their fruitfulness will be enhanced.

Just as the branch cannot bear fruit without the vine the disciple cannot bear fruit without the Spirit of Christ. As his followers bore fruit God Himself was glorified. As God had loved Jesus so Jesus loved

I am the true vine

John 15:1-11

1 "I am the true vine, and my Father is the vinedresser. 2 Every branch of mine that bears no fruit, he takes away, and every branch that does bear fruit he prunes, that it may bear more fruit. 3 You are already made clean by the word which I have spoken to you. 4 Abide in me, and I in you. As the branch cannot bear fruit by itself, unless it abides in the vine, neither can you, unless you abide in me. 5 I am the vine, you are the branches. He who abides in me, and I in him, he it is that bears much fruit, for apart from me you can do nothing. 6 If a man does not abide in me, he is cast forth as a branch and withers; and the branches are gathered, thrown into the fire and burned. 7 If you abide in me, and my words abide in you, ask whatever you will, and it shall be done for you. 8 By this my Father is glorified,

that you bear much fruit, and so prove to be my disciples. [9] As the Father has loved me, so have I loved you; abide in my love. [10] If you keep my commandments, you will abide in my love, just as I have kept my Father's commandments and abide in his love. [11] These things I have spoken to you, that my joy may be in you, and that your joy may be full.

You are my friends if you do what I command you.

John 15:12-17
[12] "This is my commandment, that you love one another as I have loved you. [13] Greater love has no man than this, that a man lay down his life for his friends. [14] You are my friends if you do what I command you. [15] No longer do I call you servants, for the servant does not know what his master is doing; but I have called you friends, for all that I have heard from my Father I have made known to you. [16] You did not choose me, but I chose you and appointed you that you should go and bear fruit and that your fruit should abide; so that whatever you ask the Father in my name, he may give it to you. [17] This I command you, to love one another.

his disciple. If the disciple is to prove his love for Jesus, he would keep the commandments of Jesus just as Jesus had kept the commandments of God.

Keeping Jesus' commandments keeps one abiding in his love.

You are my friends if you do what I command you.

John 15:12-17

Comment
Jesus was speaking directly to his Inner-Circle and indirectly to all who called him Lord. The greatest act of love an individual can do is to lay his life down for his friend. The disciples were then elevated to the rank of friend. The Inner-Circle may have thought they had chosen Jesus, but the truth was he chose them.

Jesus then promised, "Whatever you ask in the Father's name, He will give it to you."

If the world hates you, know that it has hated me

John 15:18-27

18 "If the world hates you, know that it has hated me before it hated you. 19 If you were of the world, the world would love its own; but because you are not of the world, but I chose you out of the world, therefore the world hates you. 20 Remember the word that I said to you, 'A servant is not greater than his master.' If they persecuted me, they will persecute you; if they kept my word, they will keep yours also. 21 But all this they will do to you on my account, because they do not know him who sent me. 22 If I had not come and spoken to them, they would not have sin; but now they have no excuse for their sin. 23 He who hates me hates my Father also. 24 If I had not done among them the works which no one else did, they would not have sin; but now they have seen and hated both me and my Father. 25 It is to fulfil the word that is written in their law, 'They hated me without a cause.' 26 But when the Counselor comes, whom I shall send to you from the Father, even the Spirit of truth, who proceeds from the Father, he will bear witness to me; 27 and you also are witnesses, because you have been with me from the beginning.

If the world hates you, know that it has hated me

John 15:18-27

Comment

Jesus said the world hates you because you love me. The apostle Paul later would say, "You are in the world, but not of the world." Being different in this way is a good thing.

"You are not greater than me," said Jesus. "They will persecute me, and in turn they will persecute you. Those who trust in me will also trust in you. If they had trusted God they would not persecute me or you," said Jesus.

When salvation is present one does not have to perish. Rejection of the Christ seals one's fate. When the Counselor comes he will bear witness to Jesus. The Inner-Circle were eyewitnesses to all that Jesus said and did.

The reference in verse 25 comes from Psalms 35:19-21.

19 *Let not those rejoice over me who are wrongfully my foes, and let not those wink the eye who hate me without cause.*
20 *For they do not speak peace, but against those who are quiet in the land they conceive words of deceit.*
21 *They open wide their mouths against me; they say, "Aha, Aha! our eyes have seen it!"*

When their hour comes	*When their hour comes*
John 16:1-11	**John 16:1-11**
1 "I have said all this to you to keep you from falling away. 2 They will put you out of the synagogues; indeed, the hour is coming when whoever kills you will think he is offering service to God. 3 And they will do this because they have not known the Father, nor me. 4 But I have said these things to you, that when their hour comes you may remember that I told you of them. I did not say these things to you from the beginning, because I was with you.5 But now I am going to him who sent me; yet none of you asks me, 'Where are you going?' 6 But because I have said these things to you, sorrow has filled your hearts. 7 Nevertheless I tell you the truth: it is to your advantage that I go away, for if I do not go away, the Counselor will not come to you; but if I go, I will send him to you. 8 And when he comes, he will convince the world concerning sin and	**Comment** Jesus knew that without pre-knowledge, the Inner-Circle would have been unable to stand fast in the midst of the devastating blows that would soon have to be endured. Misguided zeal would lead to much heartbreak and mayhem among Jesus' followers in the near future. The misguided would do this because they did not know the real God. It was not necessary until now for Jesus to disclose these future events to the Inner-Circle. Jesus accepted death, knowing the Inner-Circle would be greatly enhanced by the coming of the Counselor. He was coming to be with the believers in Jesus Christ in a new and significant way. The counselor would awaken the spirit of the believers to follow in the footsteps of Jesus the Master. He would awaken humanity

righteousness and judgment: 9 concerning sin, because they do not believe in me; 10 concerning righteousness, because I go to the Father, and you will see me no more; 11 concerning judgment, because the ruler of this world is judged.	to the dangers the evil one brings in the acts of sin. He would awaken in believers an understanding of the resurrection. The timeline of the Evil One now has a visible conclusion; he will be bound and thrown into the everlasting fires along with all of his followers.

Is there a contradiction in verse five?

Many scholars contend there is a contradiction found in verse five, Jesus said, "None of you have asked me where I am going?" Earlier, in John 13:36, Peter asked him Lord, "Where are you going?" Jesus knew when he told them his destination it would bring sadness to their hearts.

Since so many "obvious contradictions" have been later resolved by the discovery of previously unknown materials I have developed the viewpoint that these so-called contradictions may in fact be simply our inadequate information.

The Holy Spirit will guide you into all truth	***The Holy Spirit will guide you into all truth***
John 16:12-15 12 "I have yet many things to say to you, but you cannot bear them now. 13 When the Spirit of truth comes, he will guide you into all the truth; for he will not speak on his own authority, but whatever he hears he will speak, and he will declare to you the things that are to come. 14 He will glorify me, for he will take what is mine and declare it to you. 15 All that the Father has is mine; therefore I said that he will take what is mine and declare it to you.	**John 16:12-15** **Comment** What Jesus had already disclosed to the Inner-Circle had troubled them greatly. While he had more to tell them he knew they would not be able to accept it at the moment. The Holy Spirit, like Jesus, would not speak on his own authority but what he heard from God. The Holy Spirit would bear witness to the authenticity of Jesus as the Son of God.

Verse fifteen is a clarification of verse fourteen

In all probability, this correction is due to the cost and availability of writing materials coupled with the author's reluctance to throw away part of the manuscript and rewrite it.

What does he mean by 'a little while'?	***What does he mean by 'a little while'?***
John 16:16-24 16 "A little while, and you will see me no more; again a little while, and you will see me." 17 Some of his disciples said to one another, "What is this that he says to us, 'A little while, and you will not see me, and again a little while, and you will see me'; and, 'because I go to the Father'?" 18 They said, "What does he mean by 'a little while'? We do not	**John 16:16-24** **Comment** The Inner-Circle discussed among themselves why Jesus talked in riddles about, "You will see and now you won't see me, and going to the Father?" They just did not understand. Jesus understood what they wanted to know and why they

know what he means." 19 Jesus knew that they wanted to ask him; so he said to them, "Is this what you are asking yourselves, what I meant by saying, 'A little while, and you will not see me, and again a little while, and you will see me'? 20 Truly, truly, I say to you, you will weep and lament, but the world will rejoice; you will be sorrowful, but your sorrow will turn into joy. 21 When a woman is in travail she has sorrow, because her hour has come; but when she is delivered of the child, she no longer remembers the anguish, for joy that a child is born into the world. 22 So you have sorrow now, but I will see you again and your hearts will rejoice, and no one will take your joy from you. 23 In that day you will ask nothing of me. Truly, truly, I say to you, if you ask anything of the Father, he will give it to you in my name. 24 Hitherto you have asked nothing in my name; ask, and you will receive, that your joy may be full.

were afraid to ask. When these things began to happen the Inner-Circle would weep and lament and not understand why the world would rejoice. Jesus compared this moment to the mother about to give childbirth. When the child is born there is little remembrance of the pain that preceded it. So it will be for them.

Jesus praised the Inner-Circle because they had never asked anything in His name. Then he gave them permission to ask anything of Him and they would receive it.

No more riddles

John 16:25-33
25 "I have said this to you in figures; the hour is coming when I shall no longer speak to you in figures but tell you plainly of the Father. 26 In that day you will

No more riddles

John 16:25-33

Comment

Jesus said the hour is coming when I will no longer speak to you in riddles. Jesus would no

ask in my name; and I do not say to you that I shall pray the Father for you; 27 for the Father himself loves you, because you have loved me and have believed that I came from the Father. 28 I came from the Father and have come into the world; again, I am leaving the world and going to the Father."

29 His disciples said, "Ah, now you are speaking plainly, not in any figure! 30 Now we know that you know all things, and need none to question you; by this we believe that you came from God." 31 Jesus answered them, "Do you now believe? 32 The hour is coming, indeed it has come, when you will be scattered, every man to his home, and will leave me alone; yet I am not alone, for the Father is with me. 33 I have said this to you, that in me you may have peace. In the world you have tribulation; but be of good cheer, I have overcome the world."

longer tell them he would pray for them. But because God loves them they may pray directly to Him.

The Inner-Circle was delighted that Jesus would now speak plainly to them. They now proclaim that because Jesus knew all things they believed in him. Jesus questioned their exuberance asking, "Do you now believe?"

Jesus then revealed to them what was about to happen. Soon they would be scattered, every man to his own home. They would all leave and only the Father would remain with him.

Jesus' concluding statement is the world is full of tribulation and misery. But their hearts should not be troubled because he has overcome the world.

Jesus' Benediction

John 17:1-5
1 When Jesus had spoken these words, he lifted up his eyes to heaven and said, "Father, the hour has come; glorify thy Son that the Son may glorify thee, 2 since thou hast given him power

Jesus' Benediction

John 17:1-5

Comment
Jesus looked toward the heavens and said, "Father the hour has now come. Glorify your Son that I may glorify You." Strong's

over all flesh, to give eternal life to all whom thou hast given him. 3 And this is eternal life, that they know thee the only true God, and Jesus Christ whom thou hast sent. 4 I glorified thee on earth, having accomplished the work which thou gavest me to do; 5 and now, Father, glorify thou me in thy own presence with the glory which I had with thee before the world was made.

Greek Dictionary defines the word "glorify" as: meaning to cause the dignity and worth of the person to become accepted and acknowledged.

Jesus then acknowledged that God had given him power over all flesh. He also had the power to bestow eternal life, he then defined eternal life as knowing the only true God and himself whom God had sent.

Jesus then asked God to restore him to his original glory.

Jesus spoke these words on the way to the Garden of Gethsemane.

Holy Father,
keep them in thy name

John 17:6-11
6 "I have manifested thy name to the men whom thou gavest me out of the world; thine they were, and thou gavest them to me, and they have kept thy word. 7 Now they know that everything that thou hast given me is from thee; 8 for I have given them the words which thou gavest me, and they have received them and know in truth that I came from thee; and they have believed that thou didst send me. 9 I am praying for them; I am not praying for the

Holy Father,
keep them in thy name

John 17:6-11

Comment
Strong defines "manifest" as: to make visible or known what has been hidden or unknown, to make known by teaching. The word had come from God and the Inner-Circle had received this word and had believed!

Jesus prayed exclusively for the Inner-Circle. Jesus would be glorified by the Inner-Circle as they made him known to the world but for those whom thou hast given me, for they are thine; 10 all mine are thine, and thine are mine, and I am glorified in them. 11 And now I am no more in the world, but they are in the world, and I am coming to thee. Holy Father, keep them in thy name, which thou hast given me, that they may be one, even as we are one."

world. Jesus dreamed that all who believed in him would be ONE!

Keep them from the evil one

John 17:12-19
12 While I was with them, I kept them in thy name, which thou hast given me; I have guarded them, and none of them is lost but the son of perdition, that the scripture might be fulfilled. 13 But now I am coming to thee; and these things I speak in the world, that they may have my joy fulfilled in themselves. 14 I have given them thy word; and the world has hated them because they are not of the world, even as I am not of the world. 15 I do not pray that thou shouldst take them out of the world, but that thou shouldst keep them from the evil one. 16 They are not of the world, even as I am not of the world. 17 Sanctify them in the truth; thy word is truth. 18 As thou didst send me into the world, so I have sent them into the world. 19 And for their sake I

Keep them from the evil one

John 17:12-19

Comment
In addition to protecting the Inner-Circle Jesus had taught them, trained them, and now they were about to graduate into full-fledged active service. Only Judas, the son of perdition, (from Latin *perdere* meaning to destroy) had failed to live up to the trust. Jesus wanted the Inner-Circle to share in the joy he experienced through serving the Father.

Jesus continued to pray the Father would keep the Inner-Circle out of the grasp of the Evil one. Jesus was now ready to send the Inner-Circle into the world just as he was sent.

consecrate myself, that they also may be consecrated in truth.

I pray for those who believe through their word

John 17:20-26

20 "I do not pray for these only, but also for those who believe in me through their word, 21 that they may all be one; even as thou, Father, art in me, and I in thee, that they also may be in us, so that the world may believe that thou hast sent me. 22 The glory which thou hast given me I have given to them, that they may be one even as we are one, 23 I in them and thou in me, that they may become perfectly one, so that the world may know that thou hast sent me and hast loved them even as thou hast loved me. 24 Father, I desire that they also, whom thou hast given me, may be with me where I am, to behold my glory which thou hast given me in thy love for me before the foundation of the world. 25 O righteous Father, the world has not known thee, but I have known thee; and these know that thou hast sent me. 26 I made known to them thy name, and I will make it known, that the love with which thou hast loved me may be in them, and I in them."

I pray for those who believe through their word

John 17:20-26

Comment

Jesus included in his prayer those who would hear the word through the preaching of the Inner-Circle and their future disciples. He prayed that all his followers would be one just as He and God were one. Jesus further petitioned the Father that the Inner-Circle be with him in the heavenly realm.

Chapter 7

Holy Week: Wednesday Night

Gethsemane

They sang a hymn	***They sang a hymn***
Mark 14:26a; **Matthew 26:30a**	**Mark 14:26a;** **Matthew 26:30a**
Mark 14:26a And when they had sung a hymn,	**Comment** The accounts given by Mark and Matthew are virtually identical.
Matthew 26:30a And when they had sung a hymn,	Before leaving the Upper Room, the disciples sang a psalm.
Mount of Olives	***Mount of Olives***
Mark 14:26b; **Matthew 26:30b;** **Luke 22:39**	**Mark 14:26b;** **Matthew 26:30b;** **Luke 22:39**
Mark 14:26b they went out to the Mount of Olives.	**Comment** They exited the Upper Room, left the city and walked across the Kidron Valley and up the Mount of Olives.
Matthew 26:30b they went out to the Mount of Olives.	The Mount of Olives lies beyond the Kidron Valley and is covered with olive trees (thence the name). On this Mountain were an unknown number of small olive groves. These olive groves were independently
Luke 22:39 And he came out, and went, as was his custom, to the Mount of Olives; and the disciples followed him.	

owned mainly by small farmers. One such privately owned piece of the Mount of Olives was known as the Garden of Gethsemane. This was a favorite spot of Jesus'. It is here that his earthly freedom ended and his arrest and trial began.

"You will all fall away"

**Mark 14:27-31;
Matthew 26:31-35**

Mark 17:27-31

27 And Jesus said to them, "You will all fall away; for it is written, 'I will strike the shepherd, and the sheep will be scattered.' 28 But after I am raised up, I will go before you to Galilee." 29 Peter said to him, "Even though they all fall away, I will not." 30 And Jesus said to him, "Truly, I say to you, this very night, before the cock crows twice, you will deny me three times." 31 But he said vehemently, "If I must die with you, I will not deny you." And they all said the same.

Matthew 26:31-35

31 Then Jesus said to them, "You will all fall away because of me this night; for it is written, 'I will strike the shepherd, and the sheep of the flock will be scattered.' 32 But after I am raised up, I will go before you to Galilee." 33 Peter

"You will all fall away"

**Mark 14:27-31;
Matthew 26:31-35**

Comment

Once on the Mount of Olives Jesus made the alarming statement, "You will all fall away from me before this night is over." Jesus quoted the Old Testament prophet Zechariah.

"Awake, O sword, against my shepherd, against the man who stands next to me," says the LORD of hosts. "Strike the shepherd, that the sheep may be scattered;" – Zechariah 13:7

Continuing in the same breath Jesus said, "After I am raised up I will meet you in Galilee."

Peter interrupted, professing he would not go away even if everyone else did!

Mark and Matthew report it was here on the Mount of Olives

declared to him, "Though they all fall away because of you, I will never fall away." 34 Jesus said to him, "Truly, I say to you, this very night, before the cock crows, you will deny me three times." 35 Peter said to him, "Even if I must die with you, I will not deny you." And so said all the disciples.	and not the Upper Room where Jesus told Peter he would deny him three times before the cock crowed twice.

The Primary source

Mark and Matthew were written earlier than Luke and John so therefore I chose to rely upon Mark.

Peter vehemently insisted that he would not fall away, and so affirmed the remainder of the disciples.

The Garden of Gethsemane	*The Garden of Gethsemane*
Mark 14:32a; **Matthew 26:36a;** **Luke 22:40;** **John 18:1**	**Mark 14:32a;** **Matthew 26:36a;** **Luke 22:40** **John 18:1**
Mark 14:32a And they went to a place which was called Gethsem'ane;	**Comment** The accounts of Mark and Matthew are nearly identical. Luke has something of a different version.
Matthew 26:36a Then Jesus went with them to a place called Gethsem'ane,	
Luke 22:40 And when he came to the place he said to them, "Pray that you may not enter into temptation."	After entering the Garden of Gethsemane Jesus told the disciples to stay and pray that they would not enter into temptation.

John 18:1
When Jesus had spoken these words, he went forth with his disciples across the Kidron valley, where there was a garden, which he and his disciples entered.

What was this temptation? Scripture is silent giving us no answer.

Eight of you stay here

Mark 14:32b;
Matthew 26:36b;

Eight of you stay here

Mark 14:32b;
Matthew 26:36b;

Mark 14:32b
and he said to his disciples, "Sit here, while I pray."

Comment
According to Mark and Matthew Jesus left eight of his disciples at this point.

Matthew 26:36b
and he said to his disciples, "Sit here, while I go yonder and pray."

Jesus takes
Peter, James, and John

Mark 14:33;
Matthew 26:37;

Jesus takes
Peter, James, and John

Mark 14:33;
Matthew 26:37

Mark 14:33
And he took with him Peter and James and John, and began to be greatly distressed and troubled.

Comment
Jesus led Peter, James, and John further into the garden.

Matthew 26:37
And taking with him Peter and the two sons of Zeb'edee, he began to be sorrowful and troubled.

Jesus then moved approximately a stone's throw from them and knelt down to pray. The human side of Jesus became very evident at this point. He knew the agony that his body would experience in the near future. He did not relish the thought of his pain. His commitment overrode his fear.

My soul is very sorrowful

**Mark 14:34;
Matthew 26:38**

Mark 14:34
And he said to them, "My soul is very sorrowful, even to death; remain here, and watch."

Matthew 26:38
Then he said to them, "My soul is very sorrowful, even to death; remain here, and watch with me."

My soul is very sorrowful

**Mark 14:34;
Matthew 26:38**

Comment
To these three Jesus revealed how deeply troubled he was. He told them to remain at this spot and to watch and pray.

I do not want this cup

**Mark 14:35-36;
Matthew 26:39;
Luke 22:41-42**

Mark 14:35-36
35 And going a little farther, he fell on the ground and prayed that, if it were possible, the hour might pass from him. 36 And he said, "Abba, Father, all things are possible to thee; remove this cup from me; yet not what I will, but what thou wilt."

Matthew 26:39
And going a little farther he fell on his face and prayed, "My Father, if it be possible, let this cup pass from me; nevertheless, not as I will, but as thou wilt."

I do not want this cup

**Mark 14:35-36;
Matthew 26:39;
Luke 22:41-42**

Comment
Now alone he went a little further into the garden where he fell upon his knees and prayed, "If it is possible let this hour pass."

Acknowledging that God could make anything happen he mustered his courage, and affirmed his faith saying, "Not my will but Yours be done!"

Luke 22:41-42
41 And he withdrew from them about a stone's throw, and knelt down and prayed, 42 "Father, if thou art willing, remove this cup from me; nevertheless not my will, but thine, be done."

Asleep First time

Mark 14:37;
Matthew 26:40;
Luke 22:45

Mark 14:37
And he came and found them sleeping, and he said to Peter, "Simon, are you asleep? Could you not watch one hour?

Matthew 26:40
And he came to the disciples and found them sleeping; and he said to Peter, "So, could you not watch with me one hour?

Luke 22:45
And when he rose from prayer, he came to the disciples and found them sleeping for sorrow,

Jesus mildly rebukes

Mark 14:38-39
38 "Watch and pray that you may not enter into temptation; the spirit indeed is willing, but the flesh is weak." 39 And again

Asleep First time

Mark 14:37;
Matthew 26:40;
Luke 22:45

Comment
Returning to the three he found them asleep. They had proven they could not make one hour of vigilance.

Jesus mildly rebukes

Mark 14:38-39

Comment
Jesus knew they wanted to be strong and stay awake. Speaking

he went away and prayed, saying the same words.

directly to them he said, "The spirit is willing but the flesh is weak." Then he instructed them to pray that they would not enter into temptation. Leaving them he returned to his prayers.

Asleep the Second time

Mark 14:40
And again he came and found them sleeping, for their eyes were very heavy; and they did not know what to answer him.

Asleep the Second time

Mark 14:40

Comment
He woke them a second time and told them to pray that they would not enter into temptation.

Asleep the Third time

Mark 14:41-42;
Matthew 26:41-46;
Luke 22:46

Mark 14:41-42
41 And he came the third time, and said to them, "Are you still sleeping and taking your rest? It is enough; the hour has come; the Son of man is betrayed into the hands of sinners. 42 Rise, let us be going; see, my betrayer is at hand."

41 "Watch and pray that you may not enter into temptation; the spirit indeed is willing, but the flesh is weak." 42 Again, for the second time, he went away and prayed, "My Father, if this cannot pass unless I drink it, thy

Asleep the Third time

Mark 14:41-42;
Matthew 26:41-46;
Luke 22:46

Comment
Returning he again found them sound asleep. Jesus was more pointed in his comment on this third failure of his most best known disciples. Have you finished your nap? Are you fully rested now? Oh well, the hour has arrived, the Son of man has been betrayed into the hands of sinners.

Get up, my betrayer is here!

Strong's Greek Dictionary gives three main usages for this word Betrayer:

will be done." 43 And again he came and found them sleeping, for their eyes were heavy. 44 So, leaving them again, he went away and prayed for the third time, saying the same words. 45 Then he came to the disciples and said to them, "Are you still sleeping and taking your rest? Behold, the hour is at hand, and the Son of man is betrayed into the hands of sinners. 46 Rise, let us be going; see, my betrayer is at hand." **Luke 22:46** and he said to them, "Why do you sleep? Rise and pray that you may not enter into temptation."	1) to give into the hands (of another) 2) to give over into (one's) power or use 3) to commit, to commend

Wednesday sometime after sunset Jesus is arrested

Judas and the arrest **Mark 14:43-46; 48-50; Matthew 26:47-50; 53-56; Luke 22:47-48; 52-53: John 18:2-9**	*Judas and the arrest* **Mark 14:43-46; 48-50; Matthew 26:47-50; 53-56; Luke 22:47-48; 52-53: John 18:2-9**
Mark 14:43-46; 48-50 43 And immediately, while he was still speaking, Judas came, one of the twelve, and with him a crowd with swords and clubs, from the chief priests and the scribes and the elders. 44 Now the betrayer had given them a sign, saying, "The one I shall kiss is the man; seize him and lead him away under guard." 45 And when he came, he went	**Comment** Since Judas was an insider he knew where Jesus would probably be following the Upper Room meal. Judas knew Jesus would be most vulnerable at this point. There would be no more than the eleven disciples to be concerned with. After gathering a band of soldiers with weapons and torches he led them to the Mount of Olives.

up to him at once, and said, "Master!" And he kissed him. [46] And they laid hands on him and seized him. ... [48] And Jesus said to them, "Have you come out as against a robber, with swords and clubs to capture me? [49] Day after day I was with you in the temple teaching, and you did not seize me. But let the scriptures be fulfilled." [50] And they all forsook him, and fled.

Matthew 26:47-50; 53-56
[47] While he was still speaking, Judas came, one of the twelve, and with him a great crowd with swords and clubs, from the chief priests and the elders of the people. [48] Now the betrayer had given them a sign, saying, "The one I shall kiss is the man; seize him." [49] And he came up to Jesus at once and said, "Hail, Master!" And he kissed him. [50] Jesus said to him, "Friend, why are you here?" Then they came up and laid hands on Jesus and seized him. ... [53] Do you think that I cannot appeal to my Father, and he will at once send me more than twelve legions of angels? [54] But how then should the scriptures be fulfilled, that it must be so?" [55] At that hour Jesus said to the crowds, "Have you come out as against a robber, with swords and clubs to capture me? Day after day I sat in the temple teaching, and you did not seize me. [56] But all this has

The torches carried by the armed men lit their way while at the same time heralded their approach. While Jesus was still speaking, Judas stepped into the light of their circle. He walked straight to Jesus. The band of armed men knew the signal would be a kiss for the victim. A kiss to each cheek was a customary greeting, but Jesus understood this was no ordinary meeting.

Ironically Judas addressed Jesus as "Master." Speaking so only Judas could hear his words Jesus said, "Do you think for a moment that I could not appeal to my Father and He would send Legions of angels for my defense?" Giving Judas another opportunity to change his mind Jesus asked, "Would you betray me with a kiss?" Without response, Judas kissed Jesus.

Looking at the men behind Judas Jesus asked, "Why are you here? Have you come out to seek some desperate criminal? If it is me you want why did you bring clubs and swords? I have been with you day after day in the Temple and you have not tried to arrest me there." Jesus then alluded to the writings of Isaiah:

But he was wounded for our

taken place, that the scriptures of the prophets might be fulfilled." Then all the disciples forsook him and fled.

Luke 22:47-48; 52-53
47 While he was still speaking, there came a crowd, and the man called Judas, one of the twelve, was leading them. He drew near to Jesus to kiss him; 48 but Jesus said to him, "Judas, would you betray the Son of man with a kiss?" ... 52 Then Jesus said to the chief priests and officers of the temple and elders, who had come out against him, "Have you come out as against a robber, with swords and clubs? 53 When I was with you day after day in the temple, you did not lay hands on me. But this is your hour, and the power of darkness."

John 18:2-9
2 Now Judas, who betrayed him, also knew the place; for Jesus often met there with his disciples. 3 So Judas, procuring a band of soldiers and some officers from the chief priests and the Pharisees, went there with lanterns and torches and weapons. 4 Then Jesus, knowing all that was to befall him, came forward and said to them, "Whom do you seek?" 5 They answered him, "Jesus of Nazareth." Jesus said to them, "I am he." Judas, who betrayed him, was standing with them.

transgressions, he was bruised for our iniquities; upon him was the chastisement that made us whole, and with his stripes we are healed. – Isaiah 53:5

Jesus then addressed the band of men, "Whom do you seek? Perhaps with some hesitation, they responded, "Jesus of Nazareth." With neither fear nor hesitation Jesus said, "I am he."

At this point, John's narrative says, "They drew back and fell to the ground." This statement is open to many explanations. Were they knocked back by some unseen force? Were they suddenly filled with fear? We can only rely on conjecture, because the scriptural narrative is silent as to the reason.

Before the band could recover Jesus said, "I am he, I am the one you want let these others go." The armed men recovered quickly, and seized Jesus.

6 When he said to them, "I am he," they drew back and fell to the ground. 7 Again he asked them, "Whom do you seek?" And they said, "Jesus of Nazareth." 8 Jesus answered, "I told you that I am he; so, if you seek me, let these men go." 9 This was to fulfil the word which he had spoken, "Of those whom thou gavest me I lost not one."

Peter used his sword

**Mark 14:47;
Matthew 26:51-52;
Luke 22:49-51;
John 18:10-11**

Mark 14:47
But one of those who stood by drew his sword, and struck the slave of the high priest and cut off his ear.

Matthew 26:51-52
51 And behold, one of those who were with Jesus stretched out his hand and drew his sword, and struck the slave of the high priest, and cut off his ear. 52 Then Jesus said to him, "Put your sword back into its place; for all who take the sword will perish by the sword.

Luke 22:49-51
49 And when those who were about him saw what would follow, they said, "Lord, shall we

Peter used his sword

**Mark 14:47;
Matthew 26:51-52;
Luke 22:49-51;
John 18:10-11**

Comment
This sudden turn of events left the disciples confused as to what course of action they should follow. Several disciples asked permission to use their swords against the assailants. Before receiving an answer Peter drew his sword and struck the servant of the high priest, cutting off his ear. Instantly Jesus said, "Stop this put away your swords. He who takes to the sword shall die by the sword." I must drink the cup the Father has prepared for me.

Only Luke reports Jesus' healing the ear of the high priest servant cut off by Peter. This is an example of Jesus compassion

strike with the sword?" 50 And one of them struck the slave of the high priest and cut off his right ear. 51 But Jesus said, "No more of this!" And he touched his ear and healed him.

even for his enemies.

Only John names the servant, "Malchus."

John 18:10-11
10 Then Simon Peter, having a sword, drew it and struck the high priest's slave and cut off his right ear. The slave's name was Malchus. 11 Jesus said to Peter, "Put your sword into its sheath; shall I not drink the cup which the Father has given me?"

Witness runs away naked

Mark 14:51-52
51 And a young man followed him, with nothing but a linen cloth about his body; and they seized him, 52 but he left the linen cloth and ran away naked.

Witness runs away naked

Mark 14:51-52

Comment
The panic stricken disciples fled in total disarray. Mark tells us there was a young man, who stealthily followed the group into the garden. Unnoticed by the Inner-Circle or by Jesus, he suddenly is seen by the arresting authorities. They attempt to capture him, but he pulls free of his garment and vanishes into the darkness.

Some surmise this unnamed individual was none other than John Mark, the author of the Gospel bearing his name.

The Religious Trial

Jesus is taken first to Annas

John 18:12-14

12 So the band of soldiers and their captain and the officers of the Jews seized Jesus and bound him. 13 First they led him to Annas; for he was the father-in-law of Ca'iaphas, who was high priest that year. 14 It was Ca'iaphas who had given counsel to the Jews that it was expedient that one man should die for the people.

Jesus is taken first to Annas

John 18:12-14

Comment

With Jesus securely bound the soldiers headed toward the palace of Annas. According to Herbert Lockyer, (*All the Men of the Bible*, page 50,) Annas was appointed high priest at the age of thirty-seven by Quirinus. Luke mentions him in Chapter 3:2 at the time John the Baptist began his ministry. Annas was an astute and powerful ecclesiastical statesman. He was also the father-in-law of Caiaphas the present High Priest.

Caiaphas had already given a clear statement of his position relative to Jesus of Nazareth.

Annas sends Jesus to the High Priest, Caiaphas

John 18:19-24

19 The high priest then questioned Jesus about his disciples and his teaching. 20 Jesus answered him, "I have spoken openly to the world; I have always taught in synagogues and in the temple, where all Jews come together; I have said nothing secretly. 21 Why do you ask me? Ask those

Annas sends Jesus to the High Priest, Caiaphas

John 18:19-24

Comment

This is an independent statement of John.

Annas was the first to question Jesus. His question was twofold, he wanted to know about the Inner-Circle, and he

who have heard me, what I said to them; they know what I said." ^{22} When he had said this, one of the officers standing by struck Jesus with his hand, saying, "Is that how you answer the high priest?" ^{23} Jesus answered him, "If I have spoken wrongly, bear witness to the wrong; but if I have spoken rightly, why do you strike me?" ^{24} Annas then sent him bound to Ca'iaphas the high priest.

wanted to know what Jesus had been teaching. Jesus replied by saying he could ask any one of the many who had heard him. An officer of the guard struck Jesus for his impertinent answer. Fearlessly Jesus responded to the officer, "If I have spoken wrongly bring a witness against me. If I have spoken rightly why do you strike me?"

After that exchange Annas sent Jesus bound to Caiaphas.

Late Wednesday night the religious trial begins!

Jesus is taken to the High Priest

**Mark 14:53;
Luke 22:54a**

Mark 14:53
And they led Jesus to the high priest; and all the chief priests and the elders and the scribes were assembled.

Luke 22:54a
Then they seized him and led him away, bringing him into the high priest's house.

Late Wednesday night the religious trial begins!

Jesus is taken to the High Priest

**Mark 14:53;
Luke 22:54a**

Comment
They led Jesus to the home of Caiaphas the high priest. The entire Sanhedrin had now gathered for the pending interrogation.

Peter followed	*Peter followed*
Mark 14:54; **Matthew 26:57-58;** **Luke 22:54b-55;** **John 18:15a**	**Mark 14:54;** **Matthew 26:57-58;** **Luke 22:54b-55;** **John 18:15a**

Mark 14:54
And Peter had followed him at a distance, right into the courtyard of the high priest; and he was sitting with the guards, and warming himself at the fire.

Comment
All four evangelists state Peter trailed at a distance. John reported Peter and another unidentified disciple followed.

Matthew 26:57-58
57 Then those who had seized Jesus led him to Ca'iaphas the high priest, where the scribes and the elders had gathered. 58 But Peter followed him at a distance, as far as the courtyard of the high priest, and going inside he sat with the guards to see the end.

Luke 22:54b-55
54Peter followed at a distance; 55 and when they had kindled a fire in the middle of the courtyard and sat down together, Peter sat among them.

John 18:15a
Simon Peter followed Jesus, and so did another disciple.

Unnamed disciple was know *by the high priest*	*Unnamed disciple was know* *by the high priest*

John 18:15b-16a
15As this disciple was known to the high priest, he entered the court of the high priest along with Jesus, 16 while Peter stood outside at the door.

John 18:15b-16a

Comment
John tells us, this unnamed disciple was known by the high priest and was allowed to enter

the court. This is astounding! Caiaphas knew exactly what the outcome of this interrogation was going to be. Why did he allow one of Jesus' Inner-Circle to witness the proceedings? We are not told the answer by scripture but we are free to guess. Is it possible Caiaphas wanted this unnamed disciple to experience his lethal power and thereby dissuade the remainder of the disciples from interfering with the final resolution of his "Jesus problem?"

Peter in the courtyard

John 18:18

Now the servants and officers had made a charcoal fire, because it was cold, and they were standing and warming themselves; Peter also was with them, standing and warming himself.

First Challenge

**Mark 14:66-67;
Matthew 26:69;
Luke 22:56;
John 18:17a**

Mark 14:66-67

66 And as Peter was below in the courtyard, one of the maids of the high priest came; 67 and seeing Peter warming himself, she looked at him, and said, "You

Peter in the courtyard

John 18:18

Comment

The arresting officers and the servants were not allowed beyond the courtyard. The night was very cold and they made a charcoal fire. Into this circle Peter cautiously ventured.

First Challenge

**Mark 14:66-67;
Matthew 26:69;
Luke 22:56;
John 18:17a**

Comment

It was not long before the first challenge was issued. One of the maids accused Peter of being with the Nazarene. Matthew records they had called Jesus

also were with the Nazarene, Jesus."

Matthew 26:69
Now Peter was sitting outside in the courtyard. And a maid came up to him, and said, "You also were with Jesus the Galilean."

Luke 22:56
Then a maid, seeing him as he sat in the light and gazing at him, said, "This man also was with him."

John 18:17a
The maid who kept the door said to Peter, "Are not you also one of this man's disciples?"

First Denial

Mark 14:68;
Matthew 26:70;
Luke 22:57;
John 18:17b

Mark 14:68
But he denied it, saying, "I neither know nor understand what you mean." And he went out into the gateway.

Matthew 26:70
But he denied it before them all, saying, "I do not know what you mean."

Luke 22:57
But he denied it, saying, "Woman, I do not know him."

a Galilean. John identified the maid as the one with the responsibility of keeping the door.

First Denial

Mark 14:68;
Matthew 26:70;
Luke 22:57;
John 18:17b

Comment
Peter was feeling afraid, vulnerable, and alone in this crowd. In response to the accusations, he said, "I do not know the man."

John 18:17b
He said, "I am not."

Second Challenge

Mark 14:69;
Matthew 26:71;
Luke 22:58;
John 18:25a-b

Mark 14:69
And the maid saw him, and began again to say to the bystanders, "This man is one of them."

Matthew 26:71
And when he went out to the porch, another maid saw him, and she said to the bystanders, "This man was with Jesus of Nazareth."

Luke 22:58
And a little later some one else saw him and said, "You also are one of them." But Peter said, "Man, I am not."

John 18:25a-b
Now Simon Peter was standing and warming himself. They said to him, "Are not you also one of his disciples?"

Second Denial

Mark 14:70a;
Matthew 26:72;
John 18:25c

Mark 14:70a
But again he denied it.

Second Challenge

Mark 14:69;
Matthew 26:71;
Luke 22:58;
John 18:25a-b

Comment
It was not long before the second challenge came. Mark and Matthew report a maid accused Peter of being with "Jesus of Nazareth." John wrote, "they" challenged him.

Second Denial

Mark 14:70a;
Matthew 26:72;
John 18:25c

Comment

Matthew 26:72
And again he denied it with an oath, "I do not know the man."

Increasingly insecure and fearful he responded with an oath, "I swear, I do not know the man!"

John 18:25c
He denied it and said, "I am not."

Third Challenge

**Mark 14:70b;
Matthew 26:73;
Luke 22:59;
John 18:26**

Third Challenge

**Mark 14:70b;
Matthew 26:73;
Luke 22:59;
John 18:26**

Mark 14:70b
And after a little while again the bystanders said to Peter, "Certainly you are one of them; for you are a Galilean."

Comment
The third and final challenge was hurled. His accuser said, "Jesus is a Galilean and your accent betrays you. You are a Galilean."

Matthew 26:73
After a little while the bystanders came up and said to Peter, "Certainly you are also one of them, for your accent betrays you."

Luke 22:59
And after an interval of about an hour still another insisted, saying, "Certainly this man also was with him; for he is a Galilean."

John 18:26
One of the servants of the high priest, a kinsman of the man whose ear Peter had cut off, asked, "Did I not see you in the garden with him?"

Third Denial

Mark 14:71;
Matthew 26:74a;
Luke 22:60;
John 18:27

Mark 14:71
But he began to invoke a curse on himself and to swear, "I do not know this man of whom you speak."

Matthew 26:74a
Then he began to invoke a curse on himself and to swear, "I do not know the man."

Luke 22:60a
But Peter said, "Man, I do not know what you are saying."

John 18:27a
Peter again denied it;

And the cock crowed

Mark 14:72;
Matthew 26:74b-75;
Luke 22:60b-62;
John 18:27b

Mark 14:72
And immediately the cock crowed a second time. And Peter remembered how Jesus had said to him, "Before the cock crows twice, you will deny me three times." And he broke down and wept.

Third Denial

Mark 14:71;
Matthew 26:74a;
Luke 22:60a;
John 18:27

Comment
At his wits end Peter tried in vain to end the challenges. He invoked a curse upon himself if he had not spoken the truth.

And the cock crowed

Mark 14:72;
Matthew 26:74b-75;
Luke 22:60b-62;
John 18:27b

Comment
Only Mark tells us that the cock crowed twice. Hearing the cock crow, Peter remembered Jesus' words and was immediately filled with self disgust and hatred. He had done what he vowed he would never do; he had denied the Master three times.

Matthew 26:74b-75
74b   And   immediately   the cock   crowed.   75   And   Peter remembered the saying of Jesus, "Before the cock crows, you will deny me three times." And he went out and wept bitterly.

Luke 22:60b-62
60b   And   immediately,   while he was still speaking, the cock crowed. 61 And the Lord turned and looked at Peter. And Peter remembered the word of the Lord, how he had said to him, "Before the cock crows today, you will deny me three times." 62 And he went out and wept bitterly.

John 18:27b
and at once the cock crowed.

Luke gives us an addition that is hard to reconcile with the other writers account of this event. "And the Lord turned and looked at Peter." Here are some of the problems the statement invokes.

1) Was Peter in the courtyard or in the court?

2) It is unlikely that Peter would have been questioned anywhere except in the court yard.

3) How did Luke come upon this piece of information that seems to be unknown to the other three evangelists?

Perhaps John's account answers these troubling questions.

Unnamed disciple aids Peter's access to the court

John 18:16b
So the other disciple, who was known to the high priest, went out and spoke to the maid who kept the door, and brought Peter in.

Unnamed disciple aids Peter's access to the court

John 18:16b

Comment
This unnamed disciple went out, spoke to the maid, who was the door keeper, and brought Peter into the court. Without doubt, this unnamed disciple must have received permission to do this.

I believe

If my reconstruction is correct, Peter gave his third denial of Jesus and was then summoned by the unnamed disciple to join him in the courtroom. It is perhaps at this point that Jesus turned and looked at Peter. Peter realized his betrayal and left the courtroom in dejection.

Witnesses give conflicting false testimony	*Witnesses give conflicting false testimony*
Mark 14:55-65; **Matthew 26:59-66**	**Mark 14:55-65;** **Matthew 26:59-66**
Mark 14:55-65 55 Now the chief priests and the whole council sought testimony against Jesus to put him to death; but they found none. 56 For many bore false witness against him, and their witness did not agree. 57 And some stood up and bore false witness against him, saying, 58 "We heard him say, 'I will destroy this temple that is made with hands, and in three days I will build another, not made with hands.'" 59 Yet not even so did their testimony agree. 60 And the high priest stood up in the midst, and asked Jesus, "Have you no answer to make? What is it that these men testify against you?" 61 But he was silent and made no answer. Again the high priest asked him, "Are you the Christ, the Son of the Blessed?" 62 And Jesus said, "I am; and you will see the Son of man seated at the right hand of Power, and coming with the clouds of heaven." 63 And the	**Comment** The council needed witnesses to justify their desire to have Jesus put to death. Their major problem was they could not find two witnesses who agreed on the charges. At last, two witnesses came forward with a similar story. They accused Jesus of saying that he could destroy the temple of God and restore it within three days, with one not built by human hands. The chief priest then challenged Jesus to give a reply to the charge. Jesus remained silent, making no reply. With rising courage Caiaphas then asked, "Are you the Christ the son of the Blessed?" Mark said Jesus replied, "I am; and you will see the Son of man seated at the right hand of Power, and coming with the

high priest tore his garments, and said, "Why do we still need witnesses? 64 You have heard his blasphemy. What is your decision?" And they all condemned him as deserving death. 65 And some began to spit on him, and to cover his face, and to strike him, saying to him, "Prophesy!" And the guards received him with blows.

Matthew 26:59-66

59 Now the chief priests and the whole council sought false testimony against Jesus that they might put him to death, 60 but they found none, though many false witnesses came forward. At last two came forward 61 and said, "This fellow said, 'I am able to destroy the temple of God, and to build it in three days.'" 62 And the high priest stood up and said, "Have you no answer to make? What is it that these men testify against you?" 63 But Jesus was silent. And the high priest said to him, "I adjure you by the living God, tell us if you are the Christ, the Son of God." 64 Jesus said to him, "You have said so. But I tell you, hereafter you will see the Son of man seated at the right hand of Power, and coming on the clouds of heaven." 65 Then the high priest tore his robes, and said, "He has uttered blasphemy. Why do we still need witnesses? You have now heard clouds of heaven."

Matthew said Jesus replied, "You have said so." There is a considerable chasm between these two replies. Mark's "I am" gave Caiaphas all the justification he needed to put Jesus to death for blasphemy. No one could claim to be equal with God and survive. Matthew's answer for Jesus being less direct left the question open as to Jesus' own position.

Instantly Caiaphas stood up and tore his garments in a gesture of total disgust. His proclaimed loudly they needed no further witnesses to condemn this man Jesus. Caiaphas asked the court what their judgment would be for this man and their verdict was death!

his blasphemy. 66 What is your judgment?" They answered, "He deserves death."

Let the abuse begin

**Mark 14:65;
Matthew 26:67-68;
Luke 22:63-65**

Mark 14:65

And some began to spit on him, and to cover his face, and to strike him, saying to him, "Prophesy!" And the guards received him with blows.

Matthew 26:67-68

67 Then they spat in his face, and struck him; and some slapped him, 68 saying, "Prophesy to us, you Christ! Who is it that struck you?"

Luke 22:63-65

63 Now the men who were holding Jesus mocked him and beat him; 64 they also blindfolded him and asked him, "Prophesy! Who is it that struck you?" 65 And they spoke many other words against him, reviling him.

Let the abuse begin

**Mark 14:65;
Matthew 26:67-68;
Luke 22:63-65**

Comment

The religious trial ended abruptly. Those standing closest to Jesus began to abuse him physically. Luke adds they bound and blindfolded him for this mistreatment. Sarcastically they challenge him to prophesy as to who had struck him.

Chapter 8

Holy Week: Thursday - Day of Trials

**Mark 15:1a-b;
Matthew 27:1;
Luke 22:66a**

Mark 15:1a-b
And as soon as it was morning the chief priests, with the elders and scribes, and the whole council held a consultation;

Matthew 27:1
When morning came, all the chief priests and the elders of the people took counsel against Jesus to put him to death;

Luke 22:66a
When day came, the assembly of the elders of the people gathered together, both chief priests and scribes;

Religious trial continues

Luke 22:66b-71
66b and they led him away to their council, and they said, 67 "If you are the Christ, tell us." But he said to them, "If I tell you, you will not believe; 68 and if I ask you, you will not answer. 69 But from now on the

Very early Thursday morning

**Mark 15:1a-b;
Matthew 27:1;
Luke 22:66a**

Comment
The interrogation carried out the evening before was technically considered illegal. To conform to their legal position a consultation, or formal conference, was held early the next morning. Matthew reports "all" the chief priests were there. Luke says both were there implying Annas and Caiaphas. The older more senior members of the Sanhedrin, the elders, were also present.

Religious trial continues

Luke 22:66b-71

Comment
Once in chamber, they immediately addressed the burning issue, "Are you the Christ?" Jesus responded by saying, "you would not believe

Son of man shall be seated at the right hand of the power of God." 70 And they all said, "Are you the Son of God, then?" And he said to them, "You say that I am." 71 And they said, "What further testimony do we need? We have heard it ourselves from his own lips."

me if I told you. I will tell you this, from now on you will see the Son of Man sitting at the right hand of God." Had they clearly understood Jesus' meaning by the "Son of Man" they would have been more infuriated.

They clearly understood the reference of the right hand of God. It was all they needed. They needed no additional testimony to affirm the verdict of blasphemy rendered the evening before.

Judas repents and hangs himself

Matthew 27:3-10
3 When Judas, his betrayer, saw that he was condemned, he repented and brought back the thirty pieces of silver to the chief priests and the elders, 4 saying, "I have sinned in betraying innocent blood." They said, "What is that to us? See to it yourself." 5 And throwing down the pieces of silver in the temple, he departed; and he went and hanged himself. 6 But the chief priests, taking the pieces of silver, said, "It is not lawful to put them into the treasury, since they are blood money." 7 So they took counsel, and bought with them the potter's field, to bury strangers

Judas repents and hangs himself

Matthew 27:3-10

Comment
The condemnation referred to here is that of the Sanhedrin, the religious Supreme Court of Israel.

The most neglected statement, by the conservative evangelical community, is **"Judas repented!"** As a visible act of his repentance he returned the thirty pieces of silver. He verbalized his repentance by saying he had betrayed innocent blood, meaning Jesus. With callous pleasure, the chief priests and elders answered, "So what?"

in. 8 Therefore that field has been called the Field of Blood to this day. 9 Then was fulfilled what had been spoken by the prophet Jeremiah, saying, "And they took the thirty pieces of silver, the price of him on whom a price had been set by some of the sons of Israel, 10 and they gave them for the potter's field, as the Lord directed me."

Judas, now the betrayed one, threw the money to the floor and left the temple. His next act was to go and hang himself. It should be noted that suicide was the most reprehensible form of death to the Jewish people.

The Temple authorities could not put the money into the treasury of the Temple because it was tainted money. So they decided to buy a Potter's Field as a burial place for the poor. The field was in existence at the time Luke wrote.

Verse nine poses a significant problem

I can find no comparable statement from the prophet Jeremiah. However this statement from the prophet Zechariah comes very close to Matthew's quote.

10 And I took my staff Grace, and I broke it, annulling the covenant which I had made with all the peoples. 11 So it was annulled on that day, and the traffickers in the sheep, who were watching me, knew that it was the word of the LORD. 12 Then I said to them, "If it seems right to you, give me my wages; but if not, keep them." And they weighed out as my wages thirty shekels of silver. 13 Then the LORD said to me, "Cast it into the treasure" -- the lordly price at which I was paid off by them. So I took the thirty shekels of silver and cast them into the treasury in the house of the LORD. – Zechariah 11:10-13

What do we know about Judas?

We know the following about Judas:

- He was the son of a man by the name Iscariot.

- His name first appears at the naming of the original twelve.

- He held the only a specific office among the Inner-Circle, he was keeper of the money box as stated in John 13:29.

- He was critical of what he believed to be extravagant waste.

- At the Last Supper his place was probably at the left of Jesus.

- He betrayed Jesus for thirty pieces of silver.

- He led the arresting authorities to Jesus in the Garden of Gethsemane.

- When he learned the Sanhedrin had rendered a verdict of blasphemy and ordered the death sentence, he REPENTED as stated in Matthew 27:3.

- He tried to return the thirty pieces of silver.

- He hanged himself.

- The writer John called him a thief.

- All four evangelists identify him as the betrayer of Jesus of Nazareth.

- He is one of the most widely known members of the Inner-Circle.

There are many things that we do not know about Judas.

- We do not know his motives.

- Why did Jesus select him as a member of the Inner-Circle?

- Was there some particular quality about Judas that Jesus saw?

- In the end Jesus remarked that not one of his Inner-Circle had been lost except the one that was to fulfill scripture found in John 17:12.

- Could it be Judas was following the will of God by being the one who would betray Jesus and open the way to the cross? Was this God's plan to bring redemption to all humanity?

- Is it possible that in the betrayal Judas saw it not as betraying Jesus but rather launching him into his full-fledged Messiahship? Since the Council did not have the power to execute, there was no reason for Judas to think that Jesus would be put to death. Was he trying to force Jesus to use some of his miraculous power to drive out the Romans and establish Jewish law for good and eternity?

- Concerning Judas returning the ill-gotten gain: Is it possible he thought he could undo what he had done? The temple authorities looked upon the thirty pieces of silver as blood money, therefore it was unclean and its presence would contaminate the Temple. So they put it to a good use for the community, they bought a piece of ground and used it as a cemetery for the indigents and those who had no property. Could it be that Judas acknowledged he had sinned and tried to make restitution of the money to obtain forgiveness?

Jesus is taken to Pilate **Mark 15:1c; Matthew 27:2; Luke 23:1; John 18:28a;**	*Jesus is taken to Pilate* **Mark 15:1c; Matthew 27:2; Luke 23:1; John 18:28a;**
Mark 15:1c and they bound Jesus and led him away and delivered him to Pilate. **Matthew 27:2** and they bound him and led him away and delivered him to Pilate the governor. **Luke 23:1** Then the whole company of them arose, and brought him before Pilate. **John 18:28a** Then they led Jesus from the house of Ca'iaphas to the praetorium.	**Comment** Having reached their verdict they went to convince Pilate to order the death sentence for Jesus. John tells us specifically that it was to the hall of judgment, the praetorium, they delivered Jesus.

Location of the Praetorium

"The Antonia, the palace/ Fortress initially described by the ancient Jewish historian Josephus at the northwest corner of the Herodian Temple Mount, is not mentioned by name in the New Testament. For a long time, however, it was thought to be the 'praetorium' where Pilate questioned Jesus and found him innocent.

The praetorium is also mentioned in Mark 15:15-16, where Pilate, to satisfy the crowd, delivered Jesus to be crucified, and the soldiers lead him away, taking him 'inside the palace (that is the praetorium).' And in Matthew 27:27, the soldiers take Jesus into the 'praetorium,' where he is mocked and hailed as King of the Jews.

The praetorium was originally the residence of the provincial governor. These New Testament references make it clear that the praetorium they are referring to is part of a palace that is a royal residence. Herod's palace was not near the Temple Mount. Scholars are generally agreed that it lay on the western edge of the city, south of today's Java date. It no doubt stood just as Herod had built it until the Roman destruction of Jerusalem in 70 A.D. Josephus describes the layout in his account of the First Jewish Revolt against the Romans. It would be and was an ideal and honorable place to house the Roman authority. ... In short, the praetorium was most likely located in Herod's palace, not the Antonia, and there is no New Testament reference to Jesus in connection with the Antonia.

Josephus tells us the Antonia was built on a high rock 50 cubits high and all sides precipitous ... This rock was covered from its base upwards with smooth flagstones, both for ornament and in order that anyone attempting to ascend or descend it might slip off.

At the top of the rock was a wall three cubits high, behind which was the 'majestic' edifice. It resembled a palace in its spaciousness and appointments, being divided into apartments of every description and for every purpose, including cloisters, baths and broad courtyards for the accommodation of the troops; so that from its possession, of all conveniences it seemed a town; from its magnificence, a palace."
(*Biblical Archaeological Review*, January/February 2009 pages 45-46.)

The Political Trial Begins	***The Political Trial Begins***
Mark 15:2; **Matthew 27:11;** **Luke 23:3**	**Mark 15:2;** **Matthew 27:11;** **Luke 23:3**
Mark 15:2 And Pilate asked him, "Are you the King of the Jews?" And he answered him, "You have said so."	**Comment** To Pilate it was an amusing question, "Are you the king of the Jews?" Caesar had not granted anyone the title of "King of Judea" therefore Jesus could not be a king in the Roman Empire. Jesus response was forthcoming, "You have said so."
Matthew 27:11 Now Jesus stood before the governor; and the governor asked him, "Are you the King	

of the Jews?" Jesus said, "You have said so."

Luke 23:3
And Pilate asked him, "Are you the King of the Jews?" And he answered him, "You have said so."

The Jews did not enter the Praetorium

John 18:28b-30
It was early. They themselves did not enter the praetorium, so that they might not be defiled, but might eat the passover. ^{29} So Pilate went out to them and said, "What accusation do you bring against this man?" ^{30} They answered him, "If this man were not an evildoer, we would not have handed him over."

The Jews did not enter the Praetorium

John 18:28b-30

Comment
The judgment hall, the praetorium, was part of a palace occupied by the Romans, (Gentiles). To enter any dwelling inhabited by gentiles would render a Jew ritually unclean. One who had not been cleansed could not participate in eating the Passover celebration. So the Jews who brought Jesus to Pilate remained outside while Pilate proceeded with his first interrogation of Jesus.

Knowing the Jewish tradition, Pilate paid them the courtesy of coming out to them. His question was simple and to the point, "What accusation do you bring against this man?"

They responded with an inflammatory and disrespectful statement, "If this man were not an evildoer, we would not have handed him over."

Pilate sees no reason to get involved

John 18:31-32
31 Pilate said to them, "Take him yourselves and judge him by your own law." The Jews said to him, "It is not lawful for us to put any man to death." 32 This was to fulfil the word which Jesus had spoken to show by what death he was to die.

More Accusations

**Mark 15:3-5;
Matthew 27:12-14;
Luke 23:2**

Mark 15:3-5
3 And the chief priests accused him of many things. 4 And Pilate again asked him, "Have you no answer to make? See how many charges they bring against you." 5 But Jesus made no further answer, so that Pilate wondered.

Matthew 27:12-14
12 But when he was accused by the chief priests and elders, he made no answer. 13 Then Pilate said to him, "Do you not hear how many things they testify

Pilate sees no reason to get involved

John 18:31-32

Comment
Pilate, somewhat angered by this show of disrespect declared, "Then take him and judge him yourself!" Defensively they responded, "We want you to proclaim a verdict of death, because we do not have the power to put him to death."

More Accusations

**Mark 15:3-5;
Matthew 27:12-14;
Luke 23:2**

Comment
These accusations are not fully detailed for us. Luke referred to only two examples, "Forbidding us to give tribute to Caesar, and saying he is Christ a king." Without doubt more were included like the laws concerning cleanliness, foods, and surely the Sabbath.

Pilate was amazed that Jesus refused to rebuff even one of the charges.

against you?" 14 But he gave him no answer, not even to a single charge; so that the governor wondered greatly.

Luke 23:2
And they began to accuse him, saying, "We found this man perverting our nation, and forbidding us to give tribute to Caesar, and saying that he himself is Christ a king."

Pilates' first verdict

Luke 23:4-5
4 And Pilate said to the chief priests and the multitudes, "I find no crime in this man." 5 But they were urgent, saying, "He stirs up the people, teaching throughout all Judea, from Galilee even to this place."

Jesus is a Galilean

Luke 23:6-7
6 When Pilate heard this, he asked whether the man was a Galilean. 7 And when he learned that he

Pilates' first verdict

Luke 23:4-5

Comment
Pilate saw at once this was purely a religious dispute. The only charge that would have concerned Pilate was the claim that Jesus was telling people not to pay their taxes. Even this infraction was not sufficient to entice him to become embroiled in their internal arguments.

He became very interested when he heard that Jesus was a Galilean.

Jesus is a Galilean

Luke 23:6-7

Comment
Suddenly Pilate's interest was

belonged to Herod's jurisdiction, he sent him over to Herod, who was himself in Jerusalem at that time.

captured. He would dispatch this quarrel to Herod Antipas. He had no doubt Herod would find just as he had. Herod could then dismiss the case and Pilate would escape another conflict with Caiaphas.

Pilate sends Jesus to Herod

Luke 23:8-10
8 When Herod saw Jesus, he was very glad, for he had long desired to see him, because he had heard about him, and he was hoping to see some sign done by him. 9 So he questioned him at some length; but he made no answer. 10 The chief priests and the scribes stood by, vehemently accusing him.

Pilate sends Jesus to Herod

Luke 23:8-10

Comment
Herod Antipas was delighted to at long last have the opportunity to meet Jesus on his own turf. From John the Baptist's death he had constantly heard about the wonders Jesus performed among the poor people. Now his imagination ran unbridled as he contemplated what sort of amusement Jesus would do for him.

The questioning took a good amount of time. The chief priest and scribes watched the spectacle interrupting with many charges to bolster their position.

Jesus is beaten a second time

Luke 23:11-12
11 And Herod with his soldiers treated him with contempt and mocked him; then, arraying him in gorgeous apparel, he sent him

Jesus is beaten a second time

Luke 23:11-12

Comment
When Jesus made no attempt to entertain Herod with some sort

back to Pilate. [12] And Herod and Pilate became friends with each other that very day, for before this they had been at enmity with each other.

of miracle Herod became surly and contemptuous. Herod made fun of Jesus and his supposed power. When his amusement of disrespect and bluster no longer pleased him he turned Jesus over to his soldiers. The soldiers would have their turn at making sport of Jesus.

Before sending Jesus back to Pilate they dressed him in "gorgeous apparel" most likely provide by Herod. The ironic note to this disgrace was that Herod Antipas and Pilate became close friends.

The "enmity" probably had its roots in Herod's jealousy of Pilate's relationship with Rome. Herod believed he should have inherited his father's throne and title.

Herod sends Jesus back to Pilate

Luke 23:13-16
[13] Pilate then called together the chief priests and the rulers and the people, [14] and said to them, "You brought me this man as one who was perverting the people; and after examining him before you, behold, I did not find this man guilty of any of your charges against him; [15] neither did Herod, for he sent him back

Herod sends Jesus back to Pilate

Luke 23:13-16

Comment
Pilate thought he was finished with this man Jesus by sending him to Herod Antipas. Once more Jesus stood before him bound and accused. Pilate again went out to them and reaffirmed that both he and Herod found no guilt in Jesus. Pilate then

to us. Behold, nothing deserving death has been done by him; 16 I will therefore chastise him and release him."

softened a bit saying, "Nothing deserving death has been done by him." This left open the door that Jesus was at least some degree of a problem he needed to deal with. In an obvious effort to appease them Pilate said, "I will therefore chastise (convince him of his errors by words or punishment), him and release him.

Pilate begins the second questioning of Jesus

John 18:33-38a

33 Pilate entered the praetorium again and called Jesus, and said to him, "Are you the King of the Jews?" 34 Jesus answered, "Do you say this of your own accord, or did others say it to you about me?" 35 Pilate answered, "Am I a Jew? Your own nation and the chief priests have handed you over to me; what have you done?" 36 Jesus answered, "My kingship is not of this world; if my kingship were of this world, my servants would fight, that I might not be handed over to the Jews; but my kingship is not from the world." 37 Pilate said to him, "So you are a king?" Jesus answered, "You say that I am a king. For this I was born, and for this I have come into the world, to bear witness to the truth. Every one who is of the truth hears my

Pilate begins the second questioning of Jesus

John 18:33-38a

Comment

Pilate returned to the praetorian and called the guards to bring Jesus to him. Once more he queried, "Are you the King of the Jews?" Jesus' answer was not pleasing to Pilate. "Are you asking this or did someone else say it about me?" Pilate answered with a tone of irritation, "Am I a Jew?" Jesus and Pilate both knew that he was not a Jew. The question Pilate asked meant that regardless of what claim Jesus made about being King it did not apply to him. Pilate wanted to know just what Jesus had done that the chief priest was so anxious to have him put to death.

Jesus responded to Pilate saying

voice." [38] Pilate said to him, "What is truth?"

if his kingship had been an earthly kingship his followers would have put up a fight. But since his kingship was not of this world his followers did not fight to defend him.

Pilate still tried to get Jesus to confess that he claimed to be the King of the Jews. Jesus responded, "Is that what you say?" Jesus further told him that He had been born into this world to testify to the truth. Pilate then asked his classic question, "What is truth?"

Release one prisoner

Mark 15:6-14;
Matthew 27:15-23;
Luke 23:18-25a;
John 18:38b-40

Release one prisoner

Mark 15:6-15;
Matthew 27:15-23;
Luke 23:18-25a;
John 18:38b-40

Mark 15:6-14

[6] Now at the feast he used to release for them one prisoner for whom they asked. [7] And among the rebels in prison, who had committed murder in the insurrection, there was a man called Barab'bas. [8] And the crowd came up and began to ask Pilate to do as he was wont to do for them. [9] And he answered them, "Do you want me to release for you the King of the Jews?" [10] For he perceived that it was out of envy that the chief priests

Comment

Mark tells us it had become Pilate's custom to release one prisoner chosen by the people at Passover. At that moment, Pilate held a murderous rebel in his prison named Barabbas. Mark tells us that the crowd came to Pilate and asked him to release Barabbas. Matthew on the other hand, said it was Pilate who offered to release a prisoner to them.

While Pilate was sitting on the

had delivered him up. [11] But the chief priests stirred up the crowd to have him release for them Barab'bas instead. [12] And Pilate again said to them, "Then what shall I do with the man whom you call the King of the Jews?" [13] And they cried out again, "Crucify him." [14] And Pilate said to them, "Why, what evil has he done?" But they shouted all the more, "Crucify him."

Matthew 27:15-23

[15] Now at the feast the governor was accustomed to release for the crowd any one prisoner whom they wanted. [16] And they had then a notorious prisoner, called Barab'bas. [17] So when they had gathered, Pilate said to them, "Whom do you want me to release for you, Barab'bas or Jesus who is called Christ?" [18] For he knew that it was out of envy that they had delivered him up. [19] Besides, while he was sitting on the judgment seat, his wife sent word to him, "Have nothing to do with that righteous man, for I have suffered much over him today in a dream." [20] Now the chief priests and the elders persuaded the people to ask for Barab'bas and destroy Jesus. [21] The governor again said to them, "Which of the two do you want me to release for you?" And they said, "Barab'bas." [22] Pilate said to them, "Then what shall

judgment seat, a messenger came from his wife. "Have nothing to do with that righteous man, for I have suffered much over him today in a dream," reported the messenger.

The crowd was still outside, because of their fear of becoming unclean before the Passover. Thus it gave an excellent opportunity for the chief priest to stir up the crowd to demand the release of Barabbas.

Pilate decided to offer them the option of choosing either Barabbas or Jesus to be released. The crowd roared its choice, "Give us Barabbas!"

Pilate, once more trying to release Jesus said, "Then what shall I do with this man Jesus?" To Pilate's utter amazement, the crowd shouted back, "Crucify him!" "What evil has this man done?" pleaded Pilate. But they shouted all the more to crucify him! For a third time Pilate asked, "What evil has he done, what has he done to deserve death?" The crowd now more boisterous than ever demanded that Jesus be crucified!

Overwhelmed and subdued Pilate relented to their demand. He ordered the release of

I do with Jesus who is called
Christ?" They all said, "Let him
be crucified." 23 And he said,
"Why, what evil has he done?"
But they shouted all the more,
"Let him be crucified."

Luke 23:18-25a
18 But they all cried out together,
"Away with this man, and release
to us Barab'bas" -- 19 a man who
had been thrown into prison for
an insurrection started in the
city, and for murder. 20 Pilate
addressed them once more,
desiring to release Jesus; 21
but they shouted out, "Crucify,
crucify him!" 22 A third time he
said to them, "Why, what evil
has he done? I have found in him
no crime deserving death; I will
therefore chastise him and release
him." 23 But they were urgent,
demanding with loud cries that
he should be crucified. And their
voices prevailed. 24 So Pilate
gave sentence that their demand
should be granted. 25 He released
the man who had been thrown
into prison for insurrection and
murder, whom they asked for;

John 18:38b-40
38b After he had said this, he
went out to the Jews again, and
told them, "I find no crime in
him.39 But you have a custom
that I should release one man for
you at the Passover; will you have
me release for you the King of the

Barabbas and the scourging of
Jesus, and to crucify him.

John 18:38b-40

38b After he had said this, he went out to the Jews again, and told them, "I find no crime in him.39 But you have a custom that I should release one man for you at the Passover; will you have me release for you the King of the Jews?" 40 They cried out again, "Not this man, but Barab'bas!" Now Barab'bas was a robber.

A petition was required

Later tradition tells us that a petition was required for the release of a given prisoner at this season. Here we find the crow, petitioning Pilate to release Barabbas. Did no one petition Pilate for Jesus' release? This would seem to be the case. None of Jesus' followers were among those who accompanied Jesus to the Hall of Justice to be seen by Pilate.

Pilate believed Jesus had been brought to him out of envy (feelings of displeasure), of the chief priest.

Pilate has Jesus scourged	*Pilate has Jesus scourged*
Mark 15:16-20; Matthew 27:27-31; John 19:1-11	**Mark 15:16-20; Matthew 27:27-31; John 19:1-11**
Mark 15:16-20 16 And the soldiers led him away inside the palace (that is, the praetorium); and they called together the whole battalion. 17 And they clothed him in a purple cloak, and plaiting a crown of thorns they put it on him. 18 And they began to salute him, "Hail,	**Comment** Again Pilate left the Hall of Judgment and stood before the milling mob saying to them, "See I have had the man scourged." Then he ordered Jesus be brought before the people. Jesus came out wearing the crown of thorns and the

King of the Jews!" 19 And they struck his head with a reed, and spat upon him, and they knelt down in homage to him. 20 And when they had mocked him, they stripped him of the purple cloak, and put his own clothes on him. And they led him out to crucify him.

Matthew 27:27-31

27 Then the soldiers of the governor took Jesus into the praetorium, and they gathered the whole battalion before him. 28 And they stripped him and put a scarlet robe upon him, 29 and plaiting a crown of thorns they put it on his head, and put a reed in his right hand. And kneeling before him they mocked him, saying, "Hail, King of the Jews!" 30 And they spat upon him, and took the reed and struck him on the head. 31 And when they had mocked him, they stripped him of the robe, and put his own clothes on him, and led him away to crucify him.

John 19:1-11

1 Then Pilate took Jesus and scourged him. 2 And the soldiers plaited a crown of thorns, and put it on his head, and arrayed him in a purple robe; 3 they came up to him, saying, "Hail, King of the Jews!" and struck him with their hands. 4 Pilate went out again, and said to them, "See, I am bringing him out to you,

purple robe. Before Pilate could say more the crowd began to shout, "Crucify him crucify him!" With total resignation, Pilate said to them, "You take him. You crucify him. I find him guilty of no crime."

Immediately the chief priest cried out "We have a law that says He should die." These words greatly troubled Pilate and he reentered the Judgment Hall and had Jesus brought back to him.

Jesus stood silently before Pilate who then asked, "Where are you from?" Jesus refused to make any answer. Pilate becoming more frustrated said, "Why will you not speak to me? Do you not understand that I have the power to release you or crucify you?" Jesus then responded, "The only power you have over me is the power given to you from above. The one who delivered me has more sin, than you."

that you may know that I find no crime in him." 5 So Jesus came out, wearing the crown of thorns and the purple robe. Pilate said to them, "Behold the man!" 6 When the chief priests and the officers saw him, they cried out, "Crucify him, crucify him!" Pilate said to them, "Take him yourselves and crucify him, for I find no crime in him." 7 The Jews answered him, "We have a law, and by that law he ought to die, because he has made himself the Son of God." 8 When Pilate heard these words, he was the more afraid; 9 he entered the praetorium again and said to Jesus, "Where are you from?" But Jesus gave no answer. 10 Pilate therefore said to him, "You will not speak to me? Do you not know that I have power to release you, and power to crucify you?" 11 Jesus answered him, "You would have no power over me unless it had been given you from above; therefore he who delivered me to you has the greater sin."

This is my personal position

The Scriptural support for the following statement is John 19:14 and is included in the following chapter.

The events recorded for Thursday would have consumed the daylight hours. It was now late in the afternoon. Everyone was weary and tensions had already reached a lethal level. Pilate still wanted to release Jesus. These two conditions lead me to believe Pilate held Jesus over night in his dungeon in the hope that Friday, the Jewish day of Preparation, would afford him the platform to release Jesus.

Chapter 9

Holy Week: Friday - Day of Crucifixion

Personal Position

Jesus had endured another miserable night in prison. Pilate had experienced a night of restlessness. His resolve to release Jesus may have weakened under the prevailing circumstances. However, Pilate left the Judgment Hall and stated his intention to release Jesus.

Pilate tries for the last time to release Jesus	*Pilate tries for the last time to release Jesus*
John 19:12-13 12 Upon this Pilate sought to release him, but the Jews cried out, "If you release this man, you are not Caesar's friend; every one who makes himself a king sets himself against Caesar." 13 When Pilate heard these words, he brought Jesus out and sat down on the judgment seat at a place called The Pavement, and in Hebrew, Gab'batha.	**John 19:12-13** **Comment** Pilate's final attempt to release Jesus was met with a devastating challenge! If you release him, "You are not Caesar's friend!" Suddenly Pilate realized Jesus' refusal to affirm or deny the charge of claiming to be a King would be anything but well received in Rome. Now he was consumed with his own survival. Without anymore hesitation Pilate took his place upon the Judgment Seat. He was now ready to surrender to the chief priest's bidding.

It was now approaching mid-day	***It was now approaching mid-day***
John 19:14-15	**John 19:14-15**
14 Now it was the day of Preparation of the Passover; it was about the sixth hour. He said to the Jews, "Behold your King!" 15 They cried out, "Away with him, away with him, crucify him!" Pilate said to them, "Shall I crucify your King?" "We have no king but Caesar."	**Comment**
	It was now approaching noon or mid-day. Passover would be celebrated on Saturday, which was also the Sabbath, when no work was allowed. Preparing a meal was considered work. So the meal had to be prepared on Friday, the day of Preparation. Passover would begin at sunset for the orthodox community. Jesus would be crucified before Passover began.
	According to John, Pilate presented Jesus to the crowd about the sixth hour of the day.

The hours of the day in the Gospels related to our present day calculation of time.

The following describes how the hours of the day in the Gospels relates to our present day calculation of time.

1st hour = 6:00 am our time, near sun up.

3rd hour = 9:00 am our time

6th hour = 12:00 noon our time

9th hour = 3:00 pm our time

Evening = at or near sundown

According to John it was near the noon hour when Pilate presented Jesus to them and said, "Behold your King." The angry mob cried, "Away with him, crucify him." The chief priest chimed in, "We have no king but Caesar!" This was a veiled threat that Pilate was betraying Rome if he freed Jesus.

Pilate washed his hands	*Pilate washed his hands*
Matthew 27:24-25	**Matthew 27:24-25**
24 So when Pilate saw that he was gaining nothing, but rather that a riot was beginning, he took water and washed his hands before the crowd, saying, "I am innocent of this man's blood; see to it yourselves." 25 And all the people answered, "His blood be on us and on our children!"	**Comment** Realizing the danger of a riot occurring Pilate called for a basin of water and washed his hands before the crowd. This was a symbolic way of saying he did not agree with the decision of the people but he was allowing them to have their way.
Barabbas is released	*Barabbas is released*
Mark 15:15a; Matthew 27:26a	**Mark 15:15a; Matthew 27:26a**
Mark 15:15a So Pilate, wishing to satisfy the crowd, released for them Barab'bas; **Matthew 27:26a** Then he released for them Barab'bas,	**Comment** One can only imagine how galling this was to the Roman soldiers. They had a rebel, a murderer of Roman soldiers in their hands, and now they were forced to release him.
Jesus delivered to be Crucified	*Jesus delivered to be Crucified*
Mark 15:15b; Matthew 27:26b; Luke 23:25b; John 19:16	**Mark 15:15b; Matthew 27:26b; Luke 23:25b; John 19:16**

Mark 15:15b
and having scourged Jesus, he delivered him to be crucified.

Matthew 27:26b
and having scourged Jesus, delivered him to be crucified.

Luke 23:25b
but Jesus he delivered up to their will.

John 19:16
Then he handed him over to them to be crucified.

Comment
Pilate had ordered Jesus scourged on Thursday evening. As stated earlier, scourging was a preparation for crucifixion. It was not intended to kill it was intended to take all of the fight out of the person and make him easier to handle.

Simon of Cyre'ne

**Mark 15:21;
Matthew 27:32;
Luke 23:26;
John 19:17a**

Simon of Cyre'ne

**Mark 15:21;
Matthew 27:32;
Luke 23:26;
John 19:17a**

Mark 15:21
And they compelled a passer-by, Simon of Cyre'ne, who was coming in from the country, the father of Alexander and Rufus, to carry his cross.

Matthew 27:32
As they went out, they came upon a man of Cyre'ne, Simon by name; this man they compelled to carry his cross.

Luke 23:26
And as they led him away, they seized one Simon of Cyre'ne, who was coming in from the

Comment
The Romans had the right under their law to impress any person for duty. The more common application of this was to compel a non-Roman to carry the luggage for a Roman for one mile. Jesus had said, if you are forced to go one mile go with him a second mile also. So they compelled Simon of Cyrene to carry the cross of Jesus.

Mentioning that Simon was the father of Alexander and Rufus was to give a reference for the reader to use to validate the

country, and laid on him the cross, to carry it behind Jesus.

John 19:17a
So they took Jesus, and he went out, bearing his own cross,

Crowd follows

Luke 23:27-31
27 And there followed him a great multitude of the people, and of women who bewailed and lamented him. 28 But Jesus turning to them said, "Daughters of Jerusalem, do not weep for me, but weep for yourselves and for your children. 29 For behold, the days are coming when they will say, 'Blessed are the barren, and the wombs that never bore, and the breasts that never gave suck!' 30 Then they will begin to say to the mountains, 'Fall on us'; and to the hills, 'Cover us.' 31 For if they do this when the wood is green, what will happen when it is dry?"

authenticity of the story. Only Mark gives us this information.

Crowd follows

Luke 23:27-31

Comment
Luke reported that a huge number of people followed behind the crucifixion party. Where was this crowd when Jesus was on trial? Why did they not lift their voices in his support?

According to Luke the crowd was made up mainly of women. If this was the case, one can understand why they did not raise their voices in protest at the trial. They would not have been heard, and would have been driven from the court yard.

Jesus told the women not to be concerned for him, but rather for themselves and their children. He warned them days were coming that would be so bad women who were barren would be called blessed. The Jew believed the barren woman was to be pitied and a fruitful woman was to be praised.

Luke records a strange statement, "For if they do this when the wood is green, what will happen when it is dry?" I take this to mean that Jesus' Kingdom is in its infancy, and they are trying to destroy it. How much stronger will the persecution be as the kingdom flourishes?

These words spoken by Jesus on the road to Golgotha would later be read and heard as a prediction of the destruction of Jerusalem in 70 A.D.

Golgotha

**Mark 15:22;
Matthew 27:33;
Luke 23:33a;
John 19:17b**

Mark 15:22
And they brought him to the place called Gol'gotha (which means the place of a skull).

Matthew 27:33
And when they came to a place called Gol'gotha (which means the place of a skull),

Luke 23:33a
And when they came to the place which is called The Skull,

John 19:17b
to the place called the place of a skull, which is called in Hebrew Gol'gotha.

Golgotha

**Mark 15:22;
Matthew 27:33;
Luke 23:33a;
John 19:17b**

Comment
The Roman soldiers assigned as the crucifixion detail led Jesus from the Judgment Hall to either the Jaffa gate or the Damascus gate. They passed through the gate, and thus were outside the city wall. Once outside the city they proceeded to the site known as Golgotha, or the skull.

Jesus offered wine mixed with myrrh

**Mark 15:23;
Matthew 27:34**

Mark 15:23
And they offered him wine mingled with myrrh; but he did not take it.

Matthew 27:34
they offered him wine to drink, mingled with gall; but when he tasted it, he would not drink it.

The Crucifixion

**Mark 15:24a;
Matthew 27:35a;
Luke 23:33b;
John 19:18a**

Mark 15:24a
And they crucified him,

Matthew 27:35a
And when they had crucified him,

Luke 23:33b
there they crucified him, and the criminals, one on the right and one on the left.

John 19:18a
There they crucified him,

Jesus offered wine mixed with myrrh

**Mark 15:23;
Matthew 27:34**

Comment
The soldiers offered Jesus a drink of wine mixed with myrrh. This mixture had a calming, mild sedative affect on the drinker.

The Crucifixion

**Mark 15:24a;
Matthew 27:35a;
Luke 23:33b;
John 19:18a**

Comment
Then the soldiers begin the grisly task of crucifying Jesus. Methodically and with indifference these skilled executioners performed their work.

The process of crucifixion

The process would have gone in this manner. Simon of Cyrene would have laid down the cross-member (it could have been similar to a length of 4 x 4 lumber or a substantial tree limb, both of which served the purpose) on the ground. Jesus would then have been compelled to lay with his arms outstretched upon the cross-member. His arms would have been either tied down, or held down by other soldiers. Once immobilized a soldier skilled in the procedure would have taken a hammer and a large spike and driven it through Jesus' arm just above the wrist. Most modern depictions show this act as driving the nail through the palm of the hand. The palm could not have withstood the stress of the body dangling beneath it and would have resulted in the flesh ripping apart between the fingers and allowing the body to fall.

One of two methods would have been used to affix the cross-member to the up-right part of the cross. (1) If the cross was assembled on the ground, the victim would have been stretched out on the cross-member as described above. His feet would have been placed one on either side of the upright and a heavy spike would have been driven through the ankle portion to secure the legs to the up-right. (2) The second method would require a rope being tied to the cross-member and placed across the top of the up-right. The cross member would then be pulled into place, and attached to the center-pole. A small tilted platform would have been placed under the victim's feet.

The victim usually died of suffocation. This result was achieved by the victim slowly losing the strength to occasionally lift his weight to allow his diaphragm to function bringing air into his lungs. The small platform served only to give a brief interlude of relief from the pressure of the body's downward weight. Because it was slanted the victim could not gain significant relief.

The Third Hour

Mark 15:25
And it was the third hour, when they crucified him.

The Third Hour

Mark 15:25

Comment
A time conflict occurs at this point. John recorded that Jesus was not handed over to the crucifixion squad until the sixth hour that is at mid-day. Mark reported Jesus was crucified at the third hour or 9:00 am.

This is not to be considered a significant conflict. Mark's earlier hour does away with the necessity of explaining what happened during the first six hours of the morning, of which John said nothing.

Pilate's Inscription

**Mark 15:26;
Matthew 27:37;
John 19:19-20**

Pilate's Inscription

**Mark 15:26;
Matthew 27:37;
John 19:19-20**

Mark 15:26
And the inscription of the charge against him read, "The King of the Jews."

Matthew 27:37
And over his head they put the charge against him, which read, "This is Jesus the King of the Jews."

John 19:19-20
19 Pilate also wrote a title and put it on the cross; it read, "Jesus of

Comment
It would seem Pilate intended to have the last word. The inscription read, "The King of the Jews." This infuriated Caiaphas.

Pilate ordered the title to be placed above Jesus' head on the cross. He ordered it written in Hebrew, Latin, and Greek.

These were the languages of the land. All who passed Golgotha

Nazareth, the King of the Jews." [20] Many of the Jews read this title, for the place where Jesus was crucified was near the city; and it was written in Hebrew, in Latin, and in Greek.

that day could read and understand the meaning.

Crucifixion was as much a message as a form of execution. The message was, "Break the Roman law and you may wind up on a cross."

Caiaphas Objected

John 19:21-22
[21] The chief priests of the Jews then said to Pilate, "Do not write, 'The King of the Jews,' but, 'This man said, I am King of the Jews.'" [22] Pilate answered, "What I have written I have written.

Caiaphas Objected

John 19:21-22

Comment
Pilate stood firm on this matter of less importance. At this point he could care less about Jesus. It was the high priest he wanted to assert his authority over!

Two Robbers Crucified

Mark 15:27;
Matthew 27:38;
Luke 23:32;
John 19:18b

Mark 15:27
And with him they crucified two robbers, one on his right and one on his left.

Matthew 27:38
Then two robbers were crucified with him, one on the right and one on the left.

Luke 23:32
Two others also, who were criminals, were led away to be put to death with him.

Two Robbers Crucified

Mark 15:27;
Matthew 27:38;
Luke 23:32;
John 19:18b

Comment
The crucifixion squad's work was not yet complete as they had two more crosses to fill. Two thieves were next in line for crucifixion. Both of these were robbers, and one was crucified on either side of Jesus.

John 19:18b
and with him two others, one on either side, and Jesus between them.

Dividing the garments

**Mark 15:24b;
Matthew 27:35b-36;
Luke 23:34b-35a;
John 19:23-24**

Dividing the garments

**Mark 15:24b;
Matthew 27:35b-36;
Luke 23:34b-35a;
John 19:23-24**

Mark 15:24b
and divided his garments among them, casting lots for them, to decide what each should take.

Matthew 27:35b-36
35b they divided his garments among them by casting lots; 36 then they sat down and kept watch over him there.

Luke 23:34b-35a
34b And they cast lots to divide his garments. 35 And the people stood by, watching;

John 19:23-24
23 When the soldiers had crucified Jesus they took his garments and made four parts, one for each soldier; also his tunic. But the tunic was without seam, woven from top to bottom; 24 so they said to one another, "Let us not tear it, but cast lots for it to see whose it shall be." This was to fulfil the scripture, "They parted my garments among them, and for my clothing they cast lots."

Comment
What earthly possessions the victim possessed became the bounty of the execution squad.

The soldiers would not have been allowed to divide up the garments until after they had finished crucifying all the victims for that day. The fairest way for them to make the division was to cast lots for it. This is an ancient form of throwing dice.

The quote in verse 24 is found in Psalms 22:18 −

they divide my garments among them, and for my raiment they cast lots.

The verbal abuse begins

**Mark 15:29-30;
Matthew 27:39-40**

Mark 15:29-30
29 And those who passed by derided him, wagging their heads, and saying, "Aha! You who would destroy the temple and build it in three days, 30 save yourself, and come down from the cross!"

Matthew 27:39-40
39 And those who passed by derided him, wagging their heads 40 and saying, "You who would destroy the temple and build it in three days, save yourself! If you are the Son of God, come down from the cross."

Religious leaders ridicule Him

**Mark 15:31-32;
Matthew 27:41-44;
Luke 23:35b**

Mark 15:31-32
31 So also the chief priests mocked him to one another with the scribes, saying, "He saved others; he cannot save himself. 32 Let the Christ, the King of Israel, come down now from the cross, that we may see and believe." Those who were crucified with him also reviled him.

The verbal abuse begins

**Mark 15:29-30;
Matthew 27:39-40**

Comment
Golgotha was immediately adjacent to one of the main roads leading into the city of Jerusalem. It had a high traffic rate. Those coming into and going out of the city took the time to mock and ridicule the three victims hanging upon their crosses. Some even shouted at Jesus, "If you could destroy the temple and restore it in three days then why don't you just come down off the cross?" This was followed by laughter, shaking of the head, and walking away.

Religious leaders ridicule Him

**Mark 15:31-32;
Matthew 27:41-44;
Luke 23:35b**

Comment
The chief priest was quick to join the chorus of ridicule. One can almost see him turning to the crowd with his back to the cross and commenting if he is the king of Israel let him come down and then we will believe.

Matthew 27:41-44
41 So also the chief priests, with the scribes and elders, mocked him, saying, 42 "He saved others; he cannot save himself. He is the King of Israel; let him come down now from the cross, and we will believe in him. 43 He trusts in God; let God deliver him now, if he desires him; for he said, 'I am the Son of God.'" 44 And the robbers who were crucified with him also reviled him in the same way.

Luke 23:35b
but the rulers scoffed at him, saying, "He saved others; let him save himself, if he is the Christ of God, his Chosen One!"

Even the soldiers joined in

Luke 23:36-38
36 The soldiers also mocked him, coming up and offering him vinegar, 37 and saying, "If you are the King of the Jews, save yourself!" 38 There was also an inscription over him, "This is the King of the Jews."

Compassionate Concern

Luke 23:34a
And Jesus said, "Father, forgive them; for they know not what they do."

Even the soldiers joined in

Luke 23:36-38

Comment
Luke tells us even the soldiers joined in the acts of ridicule by laughing and jeering at him. Not coming down off the cross was his glory.

Compassionate Concern

Luke 23:34a

Comment
While others mocked and ridiculed, Jesus with

compassion asked his Father in heaven to forgive them for they did not know what they were doing. His prayer was not only for those who mocked but for those who had placed him upon the cross. Truly no one there fully realized what had taken place.

One Criminal harassed Jesus

Luke 23:39-41

39 One of the criminals who were hanged railed at him, saying, "Are you not the Christ? Save yourself and us!" 40 But the other rebuked him, saying, "Do you not fear God, since you are under the same sentence of condemnation? 41 And we indeed justly; for we are receiving the due reward of our deeds; but this man has done nothing wrong."

One Criminal harassed Jesus

Luke 23:39-41

Comment

This is a very enlightening conversation between the two criminals. They understood the real charge against Jesus. One acknowledged that Jesus was guilty of nothing deserving crucifixion.

This criminal hanging on his cross understood Jesus was speaking of a spiritual realm and not a king planning to challenge Caesar for his earthly throne.

Scripture called them criminals they were troublemakers, rabble-rousers, insurrectionists; what we would call today a terrorist and they were condemned to death.

One Criminal Believed

Luke 23:42
And he said, "Jesus, remember me when you come into your kingdom."

One Criminal Believed

Comment

Luke 23:42

One criminal pleaded, "Jesus, remember me when you come into your kingdom." There was no joy in his today, the mob howled at him, laughing at his horror, insensitive to his pain or his predicament.

He probably was thinking at least of some distant time. Truly he was thinking about his tomorrow.

Request Granted

Luke 23:43
And he said to him, "Truly, I say to you, today you will be with me in Paradise."

Request Granted

Luke 23:43

Comment
What a difference from what he expected, and what those around him felt would be Jesus' response. The criminal's thoughts of a future suddenly became a present promise from Jesus.

When Jesus spoke of Paradise he was not talking about a place to go someday, but as a relationship begun that day.

Strong's Greek number 3857 gives us this explanation of the word as the criminal would have understood it. "Among the Persians a grand enclosure or preserve, hunting ground, park, shady and well watered, in which wild animals were kept for the hunt; it was enclosed by walls and furnished with towers for the hunters, a garden, pleasure ground, grove, park."

Mary watched

John 19:25-27
25 So the soldiers did this. But standing by the cross of Jesus were his mother, and his mother's sister, Mary the wife of Clopas, and Mary Mag'dalene. 26 When Jesus saw his mother, and the disciple whom he loved standing near, he said to his mother, "Woman, behold, your son!" 27 Then he said to the disciple, "Behold, your mother!" And from that hour the disciple took her to his own home.

Mary watched

John 19:25-27

Comment
Standing near the cross were two of the most important people in Jesus' life, his faithful disciple John, the only member of the Inner-Circle who had braved the dangers to come, and his mother Mary. There were other women there also but Jesus spoke only to John and his mother. First he said to Mary, "Woman, behold your son." Then to his disciple he said, "Behold your mother." Jesus was concerned for his mother's care now that he was departing this earthly life.

The sixth hour

Mark 15:33;
Matthew 27:45;
Luke 23:44

The sixth hour

Mark 15:33;
Matthew 27:45;
Luke 23:44

Mark 15:33
And when the sixth hour had

Comment
It was now the sixth hour. This

come, there was darkness over the whole land until the ninth hour.

Matthew 27:45
Now from the sixth hour there was darkness over all the land until the ninth hour.

Luke 23:44
It was now about the sixth hour, and there was darkness over the whole land until the ninth hour,

would make it nearly noon. An unexpected and unexplained darkness began to cover the whole area and it lasted until the ninth hour which would have been approximately 3:00 pm in the afternoon.

The Ninth Hour

Mark 15:34;
Matthew 27:46

Mark 15:34
And at the ninth hour Jesus cried with a loud voice, "E'lo-i, E'lo-i, la'ma sabach-tha'ni?" which means, "My God, my God, why hast thou forsaken me?"

Matthew 27:46
And about the ninth hour Jesus cried with a loud voice, "Eli, Eli, la'ma sabach-tha'ni?" that is, "My God, my God, why hast thou forsaken me?"

The Ninth Hour

Mark 15:34;
Matthew 27:46

Comment
At the ninth hour, 3:00 pm, Jesus lifted his head and said, "My God, my God, why have you forsaken me?" These are terrible and frightening words spoken by Jesus from the cross. These words express loss and abandonment, words of doubt. This is not what we expect from the Son of God. Strangely these burning words are words of hope. They are a quote from Psalms 22. Paraphrased they say, "Where are you God when I need you?"

Is Jesus calling Elijah?

Mark 15:35-36;
Matthew 27:47-49;
John 19:28-29

Is Jesus calling Elijah?

Mark 15:35-36;
Matthew 27:47-49;
John 19:28-29

Mark 15:35-36

35 And some of the bystanders hearing it said, "Behold, he is calling Eli'jah." 36 And one ran and, filling a sponge full of vinegar, put it on a reed and gave it to him to drink, saying, "Wait, let us see whether Eli'jah will come to take him down."

Matthew 27:47-49

47 And some of the bystanders hearing it said, "This man is calling Eli'jah." 48 And one of them at once ran and took a sponge, filled it with vinegar, and put it on a reed, and gave it to him to drink. 49 But the others said, "Wait, let us see whether Eli'jah will come to save him."

John 19:28-29

28 After this Jesus, knowing that all was now finished, said (to fulfil the scripture), "I thirst." 29 A bowl full of vinegar stood there; so they put a sponge full of the vinegar on hyssop and held it to his mouth.

Comment

Jesus said, "I thirst." John also mentions there was a bowl full of vinegar nearby. Someone took a hyssop and dipped it into the vinegar and held it up to Jesus' lips. This would be another insult to a dying man. To ask for a drink of water and to be given bitter vinegar would have been the last thing the thirsty man craved.

Jesus gives up His Spirit

**Mark 15:37;
Matthew 27:50;
Luke 23:46a;
John 19:30**

Jesus gives up His Spirit

**Mark 15:37;
Matthew 27:50;
Luke 23:46a;
John 19:30**

Mark 15:37

And Jesus uttered a loud cry, and breathed his last.

Comment

Jesus then uttered a loud cry, his head slumped forward as he

Matthew 27:50
And Jesus cried again with a loud voice and yielded up his spirit.

Luke 23:46a
Then Jesus, crying with a loud voice, said, "Father, into thy hands I commit my spirit!"

John 19:30
When Jesus had received the vinegar, he said, "It is finished"; and he bowed his head and gave up his spirit.

said, "It is finished." The last breath of life ebbed from him. His closing words were, "Father into Your hands I commit my spirit."

Torn Curtain

**Mark 15:38;
Matthew 27:51a;
Luke 23:45**

Torn Curtain

**Mark 15:38;
Matthew 27:51a;
Luke 23:45**

Mark 15:38
And the curtain of the temple was torn in two, from top to bottom.

Matthew 27:51a
And behold, the curtain of the temple was torn in two, from top to bottom;

Luke 23:45
while the sun's light failed; and the curtain of the temple was torn in two.

Comment
Simultaneously the curtain in the temple was ripped from top to bottom.

This symbolized there was no longer a separation between God's holiness and His worshipers. The curtain had always been a point of separation within the temple.

Earthquake

Matthew 27:51b-53
51b and the earth shook, and the rocks were split; 52 the tombs also were opened, and many bodies of the saints who had fallen asleep were raised, 53 and coming out of the tombs after his resurrection they went into the holy city and appeared to many.

Earthquake

Matthew 27:51b-53

Comment
This is an independent comment of Matthew that is both startling and virtually unexplainable. He said the earth shook even to the point of splitting rocks. This is certainly indicative of an earthquake. With the violent shaking of the ground tombs have been known to open as the rocks covering the entrance tumbled away.

We need to look closely at verses 52 and 53.
52 ... and many bodies of the saints who had fallen asleep were raised, here Matthew refers to persons of faith (saints) who died and were raised at Jesus' death. Matthew continues, *53 coming out of the tombs after his resurrection they went into the holy city and appeared to many.* This seems to say they returned to their state after the earthquake to come out of their tombs after Jesus' resurrection and were seen by many in Jerusalem.

Centurion Believes

Mark 15:39;
Matthew 27:54;
Luke 23:46b-48

Centurion Believes

Mark 15:39;
Matthew 27:54;
Luke 23:46b-48

Mark 15:39

And when the centurion, who stood facing him, saw that he thus breathed his last, he said, "Truly this man was the Son of God!"

Comment

The Centurion, the commanding officer of the crucifixion squad, saw all that took place and commented, "Truly this man was the son of God."

Matthew 27:54

When the centurion and those who were with him, keeping watch over Jesus, saw the earthquake and what took place, they were filled with awe, and said, "Truly this was the Son of God!"

Luke adds the Centurion proclaimed that Jesus was indeed an innocent man.

Luke 23:46b-48

46b And having said this he breathed his last. 47 Now when the centurion saw what had taken place, he praised God, and said, "Certainly this man was innocent!" 48 And all the multitudes who assembled to see the sight, when they saw what had taken place, returned home beating their breasts.

__Women looking on__

**Mark 15:40-41;
Matthew 27:55-56;
Luke 23:49**

__Women looking on__

**Mark 15:40-41;
Matthew 27:55-56;
Luke 23:49**

Mark 15:40-41

40 There were also women looking on from afar, among whom were Mary Mag'dalene, and Mary the mother of James the younger and of Joses, and Salo'me, 41 who, when he was

Comment

It is notable that the women and others were standing, "At a distance," and witnessed these events. Mark mentions these were the women who had come from Galilee and ministered to

in Galilee, followed him, and ministered to him; and also many other women who came up with him to Jerusalem.

Matthew 27:55-56
55 There were also many women there, looking on from afar, who had followed Jesus from Galilee, ministering to him; 56 among whom were Mary Mag'dalene, and Mary the mother of James and Joseph, and the mother of the sons of Zeb'edee.

Luke 23:49
And all his acquaintances and the women who had followed him from Galilee stood at a distance and saw these things.

him. Luke in an earlier passage mentioned the names of the women who traveled with Jesus and who from their resources supported his ministry, (Luke 8:1-3).

Hasten their death

John 19:31-37
31 Since it was the day of Preparation, in order to prevent the bodies from remaining on the cross on the sabbath (for that sabbath was a high day), the Jews asked Pilate that their legs might be broken, and that they might be taken away. 32 So the soldiers came and broke the legs of the first, and of the other who had been crucified with him; 33 but when they came to Jesus and saw that he was already dead, they did not break his legs. 34 But one of the soldiers pierced his side with a spear, and at

Hasten their death

John 19:31-37

Comment
The day of preparation ended at sundown and brought in the Sabbath/Passover.

The Jewish authorities were concerned mainly that Jesus might be on the cross during Sabbath/Passover and provoke a riot among the people. So they approached Pilate with a plan to avoid this potential. They requested Pilate to order the victim's legs to be broken because it would hasten their death.

once there came out blood and water. 35 He who saw it has borne witness -- his testimony is true, and he knows that he tells the truth -- that you also may believe. 36 For these things took place that the scripture might be fulfilled, "Not a bone of him shall be broken." 37 And again another scripture says, "They shall look on him whom they have pierced."

Breaking the legs meant the victim would soon suffocate because he would no longer be able to relieve the diaphragm for it to work.

The soldiers came to the first victim, finding he was still alive they broke his legs. Then they move to Jesus prepared to do the same but much to their surprise Jesus was already dead. So they did not break his legs.

One of the soldiers pierced Jesus' side with his spear to make sure that he was dead. To his surprise, and to all who saw it, out of the wound flowed both blood and water. This is perhaps a theological statement of John that the blood represented the crucifixion and death of Jesus and the water represented baptism and entrance of the believer into new life.

John then places his seal of authority upon these words. He stated that a "witness" bears to the truth of this testimony and it is written in order that others may believe.

John stated all of these things took place to fulfill the scripture that said, "Not a bone of him shall be broken." *He keepeth all his bones: not one of them is broken.* – Psalms 34:20 (KJV)

During the agony of the crucifixion

During the agony of the crucifixion the victim would begin to slump. The tilted platform and fatigue caused him to slowly strain against the spikes driven through his wrists. As his muscles cramped he used his remaining strength to stand as best he could.

In the slumped position his diaphragm was pushed into an unnatural position that decreased its functionality. The victim would muster all the strength that he possessed and lift himself up pushing against the spikes driven through the ankles gasping for each breath and some relief to his arms.

Joseph of Arimathea	*Joseph of Arimathea*
Mark 15:42-47; Matthew 27:57-61; Luke 23:50-56a; John 19:38-42	Mark 15:42-47; Matthew 27:57-61; Luke 23:50-56a; John 19:38-42
Mark 15:42-47 42 And when evening had come, since it was the day of Preparation, that is, the day before the sabbath, 43 Joseph of Arimathe'a, a respected member of the council, who was also himself looking for the kingdom of God, took courage and went to Pilate, and asked for the body of Jesus. 44 And Pilate wondered if he were already dead; and summoning the centurion, he asked him whether he was already dead. 45 And when he learned from the centurion that he was dead, he granted the body to Joseph. 46 And he bought a linen shroud, and taking him down, wrapped him in the linen shroud, and laid him in a tomb	**Comment** Evening was upon them and darkness close at hand. With night came the beginning of Sabbath/Passover and no work was permitted not even the burial of the dead. Who would claim the body of Jesus? Jewish law allowed a non-relative to claim the body of the deceased provided that party owned property in the city and would provide the burial. None of Jesus' followers owned property in Jerusalem. Joseph of Arimathea stepped forward and was granted Jesus' body. Pilate was astounded that Jesus could possibly have died in such a short time. To confirm

which had been hewn out of the rock; and he rolled a stone against the door of the tomb. ^{47} Mary Mag'dalene and Mary the mother of Joses saw where he was laid.

Matthew 27:57-61
^{57} When it was evening, there came a rich man from Arimathe'a, named Joseph, who also was a disciple of Jesus. ^{58} He went to Pilate and asked for the body of Jesus. Then Pilate ordered it to be given to him. ^{59} And Joseph took the body, and wrapped it in a clean linen shroud, ^{60} and laid it in his own new tomb, which he had hewn in the rock; and he rolled a great stone to the door of the tomb, and departed. ^{61} Mary Mag'dalene and the other Mary were there, sitting opposite the sepulchre.

Luke 23:50-56a
^{50} Now there was a man named Joseph from the Jewish town of Arimathe'a. He was a member of the council, a good and righteous man, ^{51} who had not consented to their purpose and deed, and he was looking for the kingdom of God. ^{52} This man went to Pilate and asked for the body of Jesus. ^{53} Then he took it down and wrapped it in a linen shroud, and laid him in a rock-hewn tomb, where no one had ever yet been laid. ^{54} It was the day of Preparation, and the

Joseph's claim he called for the Centurion who in turn acknowledged Jesus was dead. Pilate then granted the request ordering the soldiers to release Jesus' body to Joseph.

Another member of the council who had remained silent of his discipleship, Nicodemus came forward to assist Joseph. He brought with him a hundred pounds of myrrh and aloe mixture to prepare the body for burial. Together they took the body of Jesus down from the cross and wrapped the body and spices with linen cloths according to the custom of the Jews.

Adjacent to Golgotha there was a garden, owned by Joseph. Joseph had prepared for his own burial by having a tomb carved into the face of solid rock in the garden. No one had ever been buried there. So Joseph and Nicode'mus laid Jesus in the tomb and rolled a circular stone in place to seal the entrance.

Mary the mother of Jesus, Mary Mag'dalene, Mary the mother of Joses and the other women who had witnessed the crucifixion were close by watching to see where Jesus was buried.

sabbath was beginning. 55 The women who had come with him from Galilee followed, and saw the tomb, and how his body was laid; 56 then they returned, and prepared spices and ointments.

John 19:38-42
38   After this Joseph of Arimathe'a, who was a disciple of Jesus, but secretly, for fear of the Jews, asked Pilate that he might take away the body of Jesus, and Pilate gave him leave. So he came and took away his body. 39 Nicode'mus also, who had at first come to him by night, came bringing a mixture of myrrh and aloes, about a hundred pounds' weight. 40 They took the body of Jesus, and bound it in linen cloths with the spices, as is the burial custom of the Jews. 41 Now in the place where he was crucified there was a garden, and in the garden a new tomb where no one had ever been laid. 42 So because of the Jewish day of Preparation, as the tomb was close at hand, they laid Jesus there.

Joseph was a rich man

Joseph was a rich man and counted among the "righteous" by the Gospel writers. He had been a silent disciple of Jesus for some time. He had not, until now, publicly acknowledged his discipleship because he feared the reaction of the chief priest. The circumstances of the trial and crucifixion had been more than he could tolerate thus he broke his silence.

We do not know if this was a unilateral decision of Joseph's or if he consulted with others before going to Pilate. Joseph would have had to request an audience with the Governor; one did not just walk in and present himself.

We should remember that Joseph and Nicodemus by removing the body of Jesus from the cross, made themselves unclean by touching a dead body.

And the LORD said to Moses, "Speak to the priests, the sons of Aaron, and say to them that none of them shall defile himself for the dead among his people," – Leviticus 21:1

"Command the people of Israel that they put out of the camp every leper, and every one having a discharge, and every one that is unclean through contact with the dead;" – Numbers 5:2

And there were certain men who were unclean through touching the dead body of a man, so that they could not keep the passover on that day; – Numbers 9:6

"He who touches the dead body of any person shall be unclean seven days;" – Numbers 19:11

The Law of Moses would exclude Joseph and Nicodemus from all Sabbath rituals and eating the Passover meal. It also meant their expulsion from the Sanhedrin!

Chapter 10

Holy Week: Saturday/Sabbath

Sabbath: day of rest
Day of more plotting

**Matthew 27:62-66;
Luke 23:56b**

Sabbath: day of rest
Day of more plotting

**Matthew 27:62-66;
Luke 23:56b**

Matthew 27:62-66

62 Next day, that is, after the day of Preparation, the chief priests and the Pharisees gathered before Pilate 63 and said, "Sir, we remember how that impostor said, while he was still alive, 'After three days I will rise again.' 64 Therefore order the sepulchre to be made secure until the third day, lest his disciples go and steal him away, and tell the people, 'He has risen from the dead,' and the last fraud will be worse than the first." 65 Pilate said to them, "You have a guard of soldiers; go, make it as secure as you can." 66 So they went and made the sepulchre secure by sealing the stone and setting a guard.

Luke 23:56b

On the sabbath they rested according to the commandment.

Comment

Following the day of preparation was the Sabbath. The chief priests, Caiaphas and Annas, along with members from the Pharisees met with Pilate. They were concerned about a worrisome statement that Jesus had made, "After three days I will rise again." Even though this was not exactly what Jesus said it was the point of what he meant. They were careful to remark that he was an imposter to the kingship of Israel.

They wanted Pilate to post guards at the sepulchre for the next three days. "The posting of guards would ensure that no attempt to steal Jesus' body would be successful. If a theft were successful his followers would claim he had risen from the dead. If this happened the last lie would be worse than the first fraud," they reasoned.

Pilate wanted nothing more to do with this entire matter. He reminded them that they had guards of their own, and they were free to use them. So the chief priest ordered the tomb sealed and Temple guards posted.

Then they returned to rest on the Sabbath.

The tomb had remained unguarded over the first night.

Chapter 11

Holy Week: Sunday

EASTER

What was this first Easter Sunday like?

For Jews and Gentiles Sunday was the first day of the week. What was this Sunday like? It would become a day like no other! However; for the vast majority of people it was just the beginning of another work week.

What was the weather like on that Sunday? We have no information.

What it was like emotionally we do know. In Pilate's court it was tense, quarrelsome, and achromous.

We know what it was like for the high priest and the Sanhedrin. In the precincts of the High Priest total chaos and fear reigned supreme.

We know the followers of Jesus were cowering behind locked doors. But this would soon change. For this small band of disheartened and brokenhearted individuals, history had just turned to a new page. Jesus' resurrection opened their minds to understandings never before disclosed to humanity.

Location and description of the Burial Tomb of Jesus

For centuries the Church of the Holy Sepulcher was the only location thought to be the burial site for the tomb of Joseph of Arimathea. That is no longer the case. Many are drawn to a location more recently discovered known as "The Garden Tomb." David Longworth has graciously provided me with and has given me his permission to share with you the following information concerning this site.

THE GARDEN TOMB, JERUSALEM
(Basis for guided tour, prepared by volunteer guide, David
Longworth)

May the Lord bless you all.
June 2008

David Longworth's introduction to the Garden Tomb's beginning ,
"Welcome to the Garden!..........Our Garden is little more than 100
years old, having been developed following the purchase of land in
1896 by the Garden Tomb Association in England. The association
stills exists as a British charity, pursuing the original objectives of
preserving the tomb (discovered 1867) and its ancillary evidences,
preventing the construction of any church building over the evidences
and providing access for visitors to see the evidences and to hear
about the amazing events that took place in and around Jerusalem at
Passover time in about 33A.D.

Interest in this particular area seems to have begun in the first half of the
nineteenth century. The skull-like features of the northern face of the
old stone quarry immediately east of our Garden had been suggested
as the reason behind the name 'Golgotha' in the Gospel accounts
(*Matt.27^{33}; Mark 15^{32}; John 19^{17}*) as early as 1842 by a German, Otto
Thenius. Though controversial, as the century progressed various
strands of evidence were woven together, making a strong case for
this being the place where Jesus of Nazareth was executed. These
strands can be listed:

- The striking skull-like features in the quarry face, clearly
  visible from the northern edge of the old city
- The Sephardic-Jewish tradition that the former quarry floor
  here is the location of Beth-ha-Sekilah (the place of stoning),
  mentioned in the *Mishnah*
- The possibility/probability the Romans (having removed the
  right of capital punishment from the Jewish nation) could use
  a place of Jewish public execution for Roman crucifixion as a
  very obvious sign of their political supremacy
- The location being clearly outside the first-century city walls,
  as required by Gospel accounts

- The fact that the quarry has been cut into the northern ridge of Mount Moriah – firstly in that Mount Moriah has been associated with sacrifice from the days of Abraham, Solomon and Nehemiah, etc., secondly in that Abraham's expression of faith, 'God himself will provide a lamb..' (*Gen.22⁸*) can been seen as a prophetic foreshadowing of Christ's ultimate sacrifice, and thirdly (as pointed out by General Charles Gordon) lambs for Tabernacle/Temple sacrifices were always to be killed northwards of the altar (*Lev.1¹¹*)
- The presence nearby of a rock-cut tomb that fits several details from the Gospel accounts.

Since then, archaeology has confirmed the extra-mural position of the site (Herodian gateway stones beneath part of the present Damascus Gate). Furthermore, the convergence of the principal ancient highways to Jerusalem upon this gate position harmonizes with the statement of the Roman historian Quintilian (35-95A.D.), 'Whenever we crucify the guilty, the most crowded highways are chosen, where most people can see and be moved by this fear. For penalties relate not so much to retribution as to their exemplary effect.' (*Declamationes, 274*). That the crucifixion of Jesus took place outside a city gate is required by the New Testament in several ways:

- Matthew says that 'as they were going out they met a man from Cyrene named Simon' and forced him to carry the cross to Golgotha (*Matt 27³²*)
- Mark says was 'on his way in from the country' (*agros* – field; *Mark 15²¹*), as does Luke (*23²⁶*)
- The writer of Hebrews says that Jesus suffered 'outside the gate' (*Heb.13¹²*)

Finally, Matthew and Mark speak of 'those who passed by' (*paraporeuomenoi* – travelled near; *Matt.27³⁹; Mark 15²⁹*) and thus evoke a roadside position, such as identified by Quintilian.

However, although we present this site as a strong contender for the location of the crucifixion of Jesus, we cannot prove it beyond doubt. What IS beyond doubt is that Jesus, Jewish Messiah and Son of God truly died as a sacrifice for sin. John the Baptist's introduction of Jesus set the scene.

According to the Gospels Jesus died at about 3:00 pm (or between 3 and 4:00 pm – the ninth hour) (*Mark 15$^{33-39}$; Luke 23$^{44-46}$*). Sundown at Passover time is roughly between 6 to 7:00 pm, depending on lunar cycles. As all good Jewish folk had to be home by sundown to keep *Shabbat*, this leaves only three hours for Joseph of Arimathea to go the governor's palace, obtain an interview with Pontius Pilate, make his request for permission to bury the body of Jesus, for Pilate to summon the senior officer to check that Jesus was indeed already dead, give authority to Joseph, then for Joseph to return to Golgotha, and, with his Sanhedrin colleague, Nicodemus, (presumably assisted by servants) take the body, along with linen cloths and about 75lb (34kg) of myrrh and aloe spices (*John 19$^{39-40}$*), through a nearby garden to a tomb, prepare the body for burial, close the tomb and return home. It must have been quite a hurried sequence, and this explains why the women would have to come back after *Shabbat* with the intention of completing the anointing of the body of Jesus.

The Gospels provide many details about the burial place:
- It was in a garden
- It was close to Golgotha
- It belonged to Joseph of Arimathea, a member of the supreme court of Israel
- It was a new memorial tomb (*mnemeion*) *(Matt. 27^{60}; John 19^{41})*
- No-one had been buried there before *(Luke 23^{53}; John 19^{41})*
- It was cut out of solid rock *(Matt. 27^{60}; Luke 23^{53})*
- It was closed by a very large round stone *(Matt. 27^{60}; esp. Mark 16^4 – 'exceedingly large')*

These details match the Garden Tomb very well. This tomb is
- Associated with evidence of a garden (the large ancient cistern (discovered in the 1880's)indicates the availability of a substantial water supply, essential for gardening in this climate at an elevated location on permeable limestone; the ancient wine press (discovered early in 1920's) shows that a vineyard formerly existed at this site in the days of Jesus
- It is close to the most likely location of Golgotha
- It is a memorial tomb, containing both a burial chamber and a weeping/memorial chamber, characteristic of a wealthy family

- It is cut out of solid rock (the limestone clockwork to the right of the doorway is the result of nineteenth century repairs, following collapse of the cracked rock during excavation)
- The groove in front of the entrance indicates where the closure stone would have rolled; the height of the present entrance would have been originally no more than 4' 6" (c.1.4m), (having been enlarged in the Byzantine or Crusader periods, when the tomb was re-used). These dimensions yield an estimate of about two tons for the weight of the closure stone – a truly 'great stone.' befitting a rich man's tomb)

Jesus' body would normally have been disposed of on the city dump, or in a common unmarked grave with the rebels', but his burial was actually in a rich man's tomb, fulfilling precisely the details of *Isaiah 53⁹* – a prophecy made some seven centuries before!

And so, in our mind's eye, we can imagine the group bearing the body of Jesus moving through the garden towards the tomb as the sun was sinking toward the western horizon. Following them at a distance is another group – those amazing women from Galilee *(Luke 23⁵⁵)*. These are the ones who had supported Jesus 'from their substance' during his Galilean ministry *(Luke 8³)* and who had witnessed the whole gory business of crucifixion from start to finish. They included Mary Magdalene and Mary the mother of James and Joses (the other Mary, wife of Cleopas), Salome, mother of James and John and sister of Mary, the mother of Jesus *(Matt.27⁵⁶,⁶¹; Mark 15⁴⁰, ⁴⁷; John 19²⁵)*, and quite probably Joanna, the wife of Chuza, Herod's steward *(Luke 8³, 24¹⁰; John19²⁵)*. It seems unlikely that these women would have been able to approach the Sanhedrin members, Joseph and Nicodemus, so as the body of Jesus was prepared, washed, anointed with spices, wrapped from foot to neck in linen strips (*'othoniois' –John 19⁴⁰*) and then a separate cloth (*'sudarion'*) wrapped around the head *(John 20⁷)*, the Galilean ladies sat opposite the tomb, observing whatever they could. Finally, the great stone was rolled across the entrance and the burial party and the women departed to keep *Shabbat (Luke 23⁵⁶)*. From the later evidence of Cleopas, it seemed that the day closed with dashed hopes, the 'Jesus movement' terminated by an act of unimagined violence *(Luke 24¹⁷⁻²¹)*. It was all over.

As dawn was breaking on the Sunday morning, the Galilean women returned to the garden with the spices they had prepared the previous evening. One thing pre-occupied them, causing much concern – the great stone that closed the tomb. They had seen the effort it had taken the men to roll it closed – they knew for sure they wouldn't be able to move it an inch! *(Mark 16³)*. But during the night Almighty God had intervened. He had shaken this place with an earthquake; the angel of the Lord had descended. The stone was rolled away and the angel sat upon it. The guards were terrified and passed out *(Matt.28²⁻³)*. By the time the ladies arrived the guards had fled, the angel had gone into the tomb; apparently the ladies knew nothing about them at this stage.

It seems that Mary Magdalene must have been at the head of the group, the first to approach the open tomb; maybe her first reaction was to assume theft by the authorities and then to run and report this as quickly as possible to the apostles. Her words, as recorded by John, ring across the centuries with pure panic, brevity and breathlessness 'They have taken away the Lord from the tomb and we don't know where they've put Him!' *(John20²)* Meanwhile, the other women have entered the tomb. Luke says that they find it empty before experiencing an angelic encounter *(Luke 24³⁻⁴)*. Their first reaction (rather like the guards) is fear *(Matt.24⁵; Mark16⁵; Luke 24⁵)*, but to their amazement they are re-assured, questioned and given amazing news. 'Don't be frightened', is the re-assurance. 'Why are you looking for the living among the dead?' is the question *(Luke 24⁵)*. Now when I was a young man, having been brought up in a Christian family and being very familiar with the Easter story, I was brought up short by this question and couldn't really understand it. Here was <u>one</u> tomb, only <u>one</u> body had been buried here, <u>no-one</u> had been buried in it before. Why did the angel say '<u>among</u> the dead'? Where were they? Many years later, right here in this garden, I found the answer. To your left, as you face this tomb, in the next property beyond the lane is an ancient Jewish tomb complex with about twenty burial positions. Such tombs, like this one, were designed for re-use over and over again, with bones being collected together into ossuaries (bone boxes). Like this tomb, they, too, are cut out of the rock. Although the entrance to the complex is beyond the lane, the tombs extend eastwards, and one lies behind the rock face you can see right here, near this oleander bush. In other words we are on the edge of an ancient cemetery. Now the angel's question makes perfect sense!

Meanwhile, Peter and John are running to the garden, probably by a different route. John, being the younger, arrives first at the tomb. In his account John says that he bent down to see inside (Remember, how high was the entrance?). He records, with all the freshness of an eyewitness, exactly what he saw from outside; 'the linen strips lying (literally, lying flat, or stretched-out), and the cloth that had been around his head wrapped up in a separate place by itself' – all very orderly, and no sign of a body! *(John 20ᵌ⁻⁷)* Peter then arrives – remember, he's the older guy – I imagine him thoroughly out of breath, and maybe a little miffed that John got there first. But he's still the same Peter – impetuous as ever – no way would he stand outside and wait! Pushing past John, he entered the tomb and saw exactly the same evidence that John had seen. John says of him that 'he saw and he believed' but 'didn't yet discern the Scripture that says that He must rise from the dead' *(John 20⁸⁻⁹)*. Luke records Peter's departure from the tomb as full of amazement at what had happened *(Luke 24¹²)*.

In the days and weeks after the resurrection, the Risen Jesus spent time with many of his followers. He spoke with them and taught them many things. He shared meals with them in Jerusalem *(Luke 24⁴¹⁻⁴³)* and in the Galilee *(John 21⁹⁻¹³)*. They were encouraged to check that he was real and not a ghostly apparition; 'Handle me and see; a spirit does not have flesh and bones as you see me have' *(Luke 24³⁷⁻⁴⁰)* and, 'Put your finger here, see my hands. Reach out you hand and put it into my side. Stop doubting and believe.' *(John 20²⁴⁻²⁸)* The Gospel accounts are honest about the confusion and the doubts that naturally occurred and they show clearly how such things were factually resolved.

In the same letter to the Corinthian Christians, Paul drew their attention to the eyewitness experiences of Peter and of James personally and of the twelve apostles as a group in meeting the Risen Jesus. He also mentions something immense that is not recorded in the Gospels – a meeting between the Risen Jesus and more than 500 men – 'some have died' says Paul, 'but most are still alive' *(1 Cor.15⁶)*. This was written in about 57A.D., and it's as if Paul were saying, 'If you don't believe me, go to Jerusalem and check it out! The evidence is outstanding.' Luke, writing some years later, says that Jesus 'showed himself alive.... by many infallible proofs (*'tekmeria'* – *criteria of certainty*).' *(Acts 1³)* Peter, in his second letter asserts 'we did not follow cunningly-devised fables *(mythoi)*, but were <u>eyewitnesses</u> of his majesty' *(2 Pet.1¹⁶)*.

Some appreciable time later, possibly in the second or third century, early Christians left a mark upon the rock face to the left of the tomb entrance. Such a mark can also be seen in the catacombs in Rome. It is the combination of two symbols, an anchor and a cross. It is a simple symbol, rather like the fish/*ichthus* – full of meaning to those 'in the know' yet obscure to others. This symbol has its roots in *Hebrews 6*[19-20]. We have this hope as an anchor for the soul, firm and secure. It enters the inner sanctuary behind the curtain, where Jesus, who went before us, has entered on our behalf. He has become a high priest forever in the order of Melchizedek. By the symbol you see here, it's as if those early Christians encouraged one another with the fact that Jesus died to give us this rock-solid hope. I trust that you know this for yourselves today, and that, if you don't, you very soon will."

EASTER

Day break

**Mark 16:1-2;
Matthew 28:1;
Luke 24:1**

Mark 16:1-2
[1] And when the sabbath was past, Mary Mag'dalene, and Mary the mother of James, and Salo'me, bought spices, so that they might go and anoint him. [2] And very early on the first day of the week they went to the tomb when the sun had risen.

Matthew 28:1
Now after the sabbath, toward the dawn of the first day of the week, Mary Mag'dalene and the other Mary went to see the sepulchre.

Luke 24:1
But on the first day of the week, at early dawn, they went to the tomb, taking the spices which they had prepared.

EASTER

Day break

**Mark 16:1-2;
Matthew 28:1;
Luke 24:1**

Comment
Mark, Matthew, and Luke combine to say Mary Magdalene, Salome, and Mary the mother of James all went to the tomb. Their purpose was to prepare Jesus' body or final burial.

The problem of the Stone

Mark 16:3
And they were saying to one another, "Who will roll away the stone for us from the door of the tomb?"

The problem of the Stone

Mark 16:3

Comment
Walking toward the tomb their conversation centered on a major problem facing them. How could they move such a monstrous stone from the tomb entrance?

Problem Solved

**Mark 16:4;
Luke 24:2**

Mark 16:4
And looking up, they saw that the stone was rolled back; – it was very large.

Luke 24:2
And they found the stone rolled away from the tomb,

Problem Solved

**Mark 16:4;
Luke 24:2**

Comment
When they reached the tomb they saw their problem had been resolved for them. The stone had already been rolled away.

How had this problem been solved?

Matthew 28:2
And behold, there was a great earthquake; for an angel of the Lord descended from heaven and came and rolled back the stone, and sat upon it.

How had this problem been solved?

Matthew 28:2

Their problem had been resolved hours earlier. An earthquake struck the area. Perhaps this was an aftershock of the quake of the day before. This time, an angel of the Lord came and rolled back the stone that covered the door.

What about the Guards?

Matthew 28:4
And for fear of him the guards trembled and became like dead men.

What about the Guards?

Matthew 28:4

Comment
The guards who had been stationed at the tomb to ensure Jesus did not leave the tomb were immobilized by fear and looked as though they were dead themselves. The earthquake and the appearance of the angel was all it took to cause the terrified guards to abandon their post as quickly as possible.

They entered the tomb

**Mark 16:5-6;
Matthew 28:5-6;
Luke 24:3-8**

Mark 16:5-6
5 And entering the tomb, they saw a young man sitting on the right side, dressed in a white robe; and they were amazed. 6 And he said to them, "Do not be amazed; you seek Jesus of Nazareth, who was crucified. He has risen, he is not here; see the place where they laid him.

Matthew 28:3, 5-6
3 His appearance was like lightning, and his raiment white as snow... 5 But the angel said to the women, "Do not be afraid; for I know that you seek Jesus who was crucified. 6 He is

They entered the tomb

**Mark 16:5-6;
Matthew 28:3, 5-6;
Luke 24:3-8**

Comment
The angel sitting upon the stone told them to not be afraid. Settling their fears, he said, "I know you have come to find Jesus who was crucified." He went on to tell them he had been raised and was no longer there, and invited them to see for themselves.

Entering the tomb, they found it empty as promised by the angel. But what they saw astounded them even more. There were two more angels present.

Luke described them as "Two

not here; for he has risen, as he said. Come, see the place where he lay.

Luke 24:3-8
3 but when they went in they did not find the body. 4 While they were perplexed about this, behold, two men stood by them in dazzling apparel; 5 and as they were frightened and bowed their faces to the ground, the men said to them, "Why do you seek the living among the dead? 6 Remember how he told you, while he was still in Galilee, 7 that the Son of man must be delivered into the hands of sinful men, and be crucified, and on the third day rise." 8 And they remembered his words,

Angel orders

Mark 16:7-8
7 But go, tell his disciples and Peter that he is going before you to Galilee; there you will see him, as he told you." 8 And they went out and fled from the tomb; for trembling and astonishment had come upon them; and they said nothing to any one, for they were afraid.

men in dazzling apparel." More frightened than ever they bowed their faces toward the ground.

One of the Angels broke the tense silence, asking, "Why do you seek the living among the dead?" He told them not be afraid. See for yourself here is the place where he was laid. Then he reminded them that Jesus had said to them, while they were still in Galilee, that he must be crucified and on the third day he would be raised. Now they remember everything Jesus had said.

Angel orders

Mark 16:7-8

Comment
They were then told to go tell Peter and the other disciples that he had been raised from the dead, and was going to Galilee before them.

Quick departure

Matthew 28:7-8
7 Then go quickly and tell his disciples that he has risen from the dead, and behold, he is going before you to Galilee; there you will see him. Lo, I have told you."
8 So they departed quickly from the tomb with fear and great joy, and ran to tell his disciples.

Meeting Jesus

Matthew 28:9-10
9 And behold, Jesus met them and said, "Hail!" And they came up and took hold of his feet and worshiped him. 10 Then Jesus said to them, "Do not be afraid; go and tell my brethren to go to Galilee, and there they will see me."

The others do not believe them

Luke 24:9-11
9 and returning from the tomb they told all this to the eleven and to all the rest. 10 Now it was Mary Mag'dalene and Jo-an'na and Mary the mother of James and the other women with them who told this to the apostles; 11 but these words seemed to them an idle tale, and they did not believe them.

Quick departure

Matthew 28:7-8

Comment
They quickly departed the tomb still bewildered by all that had taken place before their very eyes. With fear and joy they ran to find the other disciples.

Meeting Jesus

Matthew 28:9-10

Comment
Before they had made it out of the garden they encountered Jesus, who greeted them saying, "Hail." Falling before him they touched his feet and worshiped him. Once again, they were told two things, do not be afraid and go tell the rest of the disciples to go to Galilee, there they would see him.

The others do not believe them

Luke 24:9-11

Comment
Luke tells us that when the women told Peter and the others of the events at the tomb they thought it was some kind of an idle tale.

<u>*John's account varies from the others.*</u>

It is known that at some point after the Resurrection John took Mary, Jesus' mother, to Ephesus where they lived for many years. Without doubt during these years Mary and John discussed in depth many of the particulars of Jesus' life and ministry.

So when John reported that Mary Magdalene went alone to the tomb early that morning while it was still dark he was using personal knowledge or that of a source in which he had absolute confidence.

John's Report	*John's Report*
John 20:1-10	**John 20:1-10**
1 Now on the first day of the week Mary Mag'dalene came to the tomb early, while it was still dark, and saw that the stone had been taken away from the tomb. 2 So she ran, and went to Simon Peter and the other disciple, the one whom Jesus loved, and said to them, "They have taken the Lord out of the tomb, and we do not know where they have laid him."	**Comment** Mary had worried greatly concerning how she would be able to move the stone from the tomb's opening. To her total amazement when she arrived at the tomb the stone had already been rolled back.
John 20:3-10 3 Peter then came out with the other disciple, and they went toward the tomb. 4 They both ran, but the other disciple outran Peter and reached the tomb first; 5 and stooping to look in, he saw the linen cloths lying there, but he did not go in. 6 Then Simon Peter came, following him, and went into the tomb; he saw the linen cloths lying, 7 and the napkin, which had been on his head, not lying with the linen	John reports Mary Magdalene alone ran and told Peter and the disciple whom Jesus loved, saying, "They have taken the Lord somewhere and we do not know where they have laid him." Hearing this report Peter and John ran to the tomb. The faster of the two, John, reached the tomb before Peter. John did not enter the tomb, but looked in and saw the linen cloths lying in the place of the body. As soon as Peter reached the tomb, without hesitation, he went in

cloths but rolled up in a place by itself. ⁸ Then the other disciple, who reached the tomb first, also went in, and he saw and believed; ⁹ for as yet they did not know the scripture, that he must rise from the dead. ¹⁰ Then the disciples went back to their homes.	and also saw the folded linens. Alongside the linens was the napkin that had been placed on Jesus' head. At this point, John had joined Peter inside the tomb. Completely confounded by what they saw they returned to report to those who remained behind the locked doors.

This exposition on the "napkin" was sent to me by a friend. The author is unknown to both of us. I cannot validate the correctness of this explanation but it is certainly worthy of consideration and inclusion.

Why was the linen cloth folded after his resurrection?

The Bible takes an entire verse to tell us that the napkin was neatly folded, and was placed at the head of that stony coffin. Is that important? Yes!

In order to understand the significance of the folded napkin, you have to understand a little bit about Hebrew tradition of that day. The folded napkin had to do with the Master and Servant, and every Jewish boy knew this tradition. When the servant set the dinner table for the master, he made sure that it was exactly the way the master wanted it. The table was furnished perfectly, and then the servant would wait, just out of sight, until the master had finished eating, and the servant would not dare touch that table, until the master was finished.

Now if the master was done eating, he would rise from the table, wipe his fingers, his mouth, and clean his beard, and would wad up that napkin and toss it onto the table. The servant would then know to clear the table. For in those days, the wadded napkin meant, "I'm done." But if the master got up from the table, folded his napkin, and laid it beside his plate, the servant would not dare touch the table, because the servant knew that the folded napkin meant, "I'm not finished yet." The folded napkin meant, "I'm coming back!"

Mary mistakes Jesus for the gardener

John 20:11-18

11 But Mary stood weeping outside the tomb, and as she wept she stooped to look into the tomb; 12 and she saw two angels in white, sitting where the body of Jesus had lain, one at the head and one at the feet. 13 They said to her, "Woman, why are you weeping?" She said to them, "Because they have taken away my Lord, and I do not know where they have laid him." 14 Saying this, she turned round and saw Jesus standing, but she did not know that it was Jesus. 15 Jesus said to her, "Woman, why are you weeping? Whom do you seek?" Supposing him to be the gardener, she said to him, "Sir, if you have carried him away, tell me where you have laid him, and I will take him away." 16 Jesus said to her, "Mary." She turned and said to him in Hebrew, "Rab-bo'ni!" (which means Teacher). 17 Jesus said to her, "Do not hold me, for I have not yet ascended to the Father; but go to my brethren and say to them, I am ascending to my Father and your Father, to my God and your God." 18 Mary Mag'dalene went and said to the disciples, "I have seen the Lord"; and she told them that he had said these things to her.

Mary mistakes Jesus for the gardener

John 20:11-18

Comment

Mary, now alone, had returned with John and Peter and was standing outside the tomb before entering. She began to weep, almost uncontrollably. Because the entrance was no more than four feet tall, Mary had to stoop to enter the tomb. Inside the tomb the first thing she saw were two angels sitting where the body of Jesus had been lying.

The Angels asked her why she was weeping. Her response was that she knew Jesus had been taken away but she did not know where he had been laid.

As she turned back toward the entrance another figure appeared, asking the same question, "Why are you weeping?" Thinking this person was the gardener she asked, "Do you know where they have taken Jesus' body?" Then Jesus called her by name, "Mary." At once she responded, "Teacher!" Mary moved toward him to embrace him. But Jesus said, "You must not touch me yet, because I have not ascended to my Father."

Mary left the garden and went to tell the disciples all that she had seen and heard and the fact that she had seen the Lord.

Mary Magdalene

Mark 16:9-11

9 Now when he rose early on the first day of the week, he appeared first to Mary Magdalene, from whom he had cast out seven demons. 10 She went and told those who had been with him, as they mourned and wept. 11 But when they heard that he was alive and had been seen by her, they would not believe it.

Mary Magdalene

Mark 16:9-11

Comment

Please take note of the following; some ancient text and versions do not include Mark 16: 9-20. I have chosen to include these verses to provide us with a closer examination of their content.

Mark and Luke (Luke 8:2) are very close in their accounts concerning Mary Magdalene.

Guards report to the chief priest

Matthew 28:11-15

11 While they were going, behold, some of the guard went into the city and told the chief priests all that had taken place. 12 And when they had assembled with the elders and taken counsel, they gave a sum of money to the soldiers 13 and said, "Tell people, 'His disciples came by night and stole him away while we were asleep.' 14 And if this comes to the governor's ears, we will satisfy him and keep you

Guards report to the chief priest

Matthew 28:11-15

Comment

The information concerning the guards at the tomb of Jesus is found only in the Gospel according to Matthew.

The guards had witnessed the angel's conversations with the women. These events had frightened them to the extent they could not move. When at last they were able to

out of trouble." [15] So they took the money and did as they were directed; and this story has been spread among the Jews to this day.

move they went to the chief priests and reported what had happened. The chief priest then assembled all of the Elders and they deliberated as to what action they should take. Their conclusion was to give a sum of money to each of the soldiers and tell them to lie. They were to answer all questions saying, "His disciples came during the night while we were asleep and took his body."

The Council further assured them should these events become known to the governor they would take care of the problem. The soldiers willingly agreed to this solution. And from that time this was the story they told.

On the road to Emmaus

Mark 16:12-13;
Luke 24:13-35

Mark 16:12-13
[12] After this he appeared in another form to two of them, as they were walking into the country. [13] And they went back and told the rest, but they did not believe them.

Luke 24:13-35
[13] That very day two of them were going to a village named Emma'us, about seven miles from

On the road to Emmaus

Mark 16:12-13;
Luke 24:13-35

Comment
On Resurrection Sunday two of the disappointed disciples were walking toward their home at Emmaus, which was about seven miles from Jerusalem. They were in deep conversation concerning all the things that had taken place that day. While they were talking a stranger joined them. This was not at all extraordinary. Everyone walked

Jerusalem, 14 and talking with each other about all these things that had happened. 15 While they were talking and discussing together, Jesus himself drew near and went with them. 16 But their eyes were kept from recognizing him. 17 And he said to them, "What is this conversation which you are holding with each other as you walk?" And they stood still, looking sad. 18 Then one of them, named Cle'opas, answered him, "Are you the only visitor to Jerusalem who does not know the things that have happened there in these days?" 19 And he said to them, "What things?" And they said to him, "Concerning Jesus of Nazareth, who was a prophet mighty in deed and word before God and all the people, 20 and how our chief priests and rulers delivered him up to be condemned to death, and crucified him. 21 But we had hoped that he was the one to redeem Israel. Yes, and besides all this, it is now the third day since this happened. 22 Moreover, some women of our company amazed us. They were at the tomb early in the morning 23 and did not find his body; and they came back saying that they had even seen a vision of angels, who said that he was alive. 24 Some of those who were with us went to the tomb, and found it just as the women had said; but him they did not see." 25 And

to get from place to place. And the roads were frequently heavily traveled.

The stranger asked them, "What are you talking about?" The question stunned them and they looked sadly at each other. Cleopas (named in the Gospel record so that the authenticity of the event could be verified) answered, "Are you the only visitor to Jerusalem, who doesn't know?" The stranger wanted to know what things. Then they began to share with him all that had happened concerning Jesus of Nazareth that day.

They said it was the chief priest who had started all of the chaos, demanding Jesus to be crucified. They told how the disciples had hoped that Jesus was the one to redeem Israel, the Messiah. Sadly they said that it was now the third day since he was laid in the tomb. They explained how some of the women of their company had gone to the tomb and found it empty and came back to tell them. Obviously, they were not among those who believed the report.

The stranger said, "O foolish men you find it so hard to believe what the prophets have spoken of the Christ

he said to them, "O foolish men, and slow of heart to believe all that the prophets have spoken! 26 Was it not necessary that the Christ should suffer these things and enter into his glory?" 27 And beginning with Moses and all the prophets, he interpreted to them in all the scriptures the things concerning himself.

28 So they drew near to the village to which they were going. He appeared to be going further, 29 but they constrained him, saying, "Stay with us, for it is toward evening and the day is now far spent." So he went in to stay with them. 30 When he was at table with them, he took the bread and blessed, and broke it, and gave it to them. 31 And their eyes were opened and they recognized him; and he vanished out of their sight. 32 They said to each other, "Did not our hearts burn within us while he talked to us on the road, while he opened to us the scriptures?" 33 And they rose that same hour and returned to Jerusalem; and they found the eleven gathered together and those who were with them, 34 who said, "The Lord has risen indeed, and has appeared to Simon!" 35 Then they told what had happened on the road, and how he was known to them in the breaking of the bread.

that he would suffer before entering into his glory." And then beginning with the words of Moses, and covering all of the prophets, he interpreted to them the Scriptures concerning himself. Still the two disciples did not recognize Jesus.

They were now very close to their town, and it looked as though the stranger would continue further. They invited the stranger to stay with them for night was close at hand. The stranger accepted their invitation. And as they served him the evening meal he blessed it and broke the bread. Suddenly they recognized it was Jesus! Almost in the same breath Jesus vanished from their presence.

They rose from the table and started back toward Jerusalem, remarking to each other how their hearts had burned in their breast as Jesus opened the Scriptures to them. Returning to the eleven they announced that the Lord had appeared to them. Then they learned that the Lord had risen indeed and had also appeared to Simon.

Jesus appears in the midst of them

Luke 24:36-49

36 As they were saying this, Jesus himself stood among them. 37 But they were startled and frightened, and supposed that they saw a spirit. 38 And he said to them, "Why are you troubled, and why do questionings rise in your hearts? 39 See my hands and my feet, that it is I myself; handle me, and see; for a spirit has not flesh and bones as you see that I have." 41 And while they still disbelieved for joy, and wondered, he said to them, "Have you anything here to eat?" 42 They gave him a piece of broiled fish, 43 and he took it and ate before them.

44 Then he said to them, "These are my words which I spoke to you, while I was still with you, that everything written about me in the law of Moses and the prophets and the psalms must be fulfilled." 45 Then he opened their minds to understand the scriptures, 46 and said to them, "Thus it is written, that the Christ should suffer and on the third day rise from the dead, 47 and that repentance and forgiveness of sins should be preached in his name to all nations, beginning from Jerusalem. 48 You are witnesses of these things. 49 And behold, I send the promise

Jesus appears in the midst of them

Luke 24:36-49

Comment

Suddenly in the midst of their conversation Jesus stood among them. It was a stunning experience for those that were seeing him for the first time. They thought they were seeing a spirit or an apparition. Jesus said to them, "Why do you question in your hearts? Here, look at my hands and my feet, it is me see for yourself, a spirit does not have flesh and bone as I do."

To further prove that he was there in the flesh he asked if they had anything to eat. They brought him a piece of broiled fish and he ate it in their presence. Then he said to them everything he told them concerning the Law, Moses, the prophets, and the Psalms must be fulfilled. Then he opened their minds that they might understand all the Scriptures.

He assured them, as his witnesses, they were to preach repentance and forgiveness of sin to all nations. Then he told them to stay in Jerusalem until they were clothed with the Holy Spirit.

of my Father upon you; but stay in the city, until you are clothed with power from on high."	

The Scriptures Jesus referred to may be located in the following list.

Hosea 6:2 is an allusion to his death and resurrection.

Prophecies, proclaiming God's glory to the nations.

> Psalms 96:3
> Isaiah 49:6
> Ezekiel 39:21

The nations will ultimately come to God.

> Psalms 67:4
> Isaiah 2:2
> Isaiah 60:3
> Isaiah 66:18
> Jeremiah 27: 7
> Ezekiel 36:23
> Joel 3:2
> Malachi 3:12

Jesus is unexpectedly there	*Jesus is unexpectedly there*
John 20:19-23	**John 20:19-23**
[19] On the evening of that day, the first day of the week, the doors being shut where the disciples were, for fear of the Jews, Jesus came and stood among them and said to them, "Peace be with you." [20] When he had said this, he showed them his hands and his side. Then the disciples were glad when they saw the Lord. [21]Jesus said to	**Comment** Walls and doors can be restraints to entry as well as barriers to exit. It was their fear of discovery that caused them to lock the doors tightly. The fearful disciples had no intention of locking Jesus out. It would take some time before

them again, "Peace be with you. As the Father has sent me, even so I send you." 22 And when he had said this, he breathed on them, and said to them, "Receive the Holy Spirit. 23 If you forgive the sins of any, they are forgiven; if you retain the sins of any, they are retained."

the power of the resurrection would truly dawn upon them. Again that evening, Jesus came and stood among them. His salutation was, "Peace be with you." They were learning the peace of Christ overcomes all the anguish the world can bring upon the believer.

Because they still had trouble believing that it was Jesus, he showed them his hands and his side. Then the disciples rejoiced as they recognized him.

Again Jesus said, "Peace be with you, as the Father has sent me so, I send you." As he spoke these words, He breathed upon them and said, "Receive the Holy Spirit." He promised them that any sin they forgave He would forgive, any sin they retain He would retain.

Chapter 12

Following the Resurrection
Before the Ascension

Thomas is not present

John 20:24-25
24 Now Thomas, one of the twelve, called the Twin, was not with them when Jesus came.
25 So the other disciples told him, "We have seen the Lord." But he said to them, "Unless I see in his hands the print of the nails, and place my finger in the mark of the nails, and place my hand in his side, I will not believe."

Thomas believes

John 20:26-29
26 Eight days later, his disciples were again in the house, and Thomas was with them. The doors were shut, but Jesus came and stood among them, and said, "Peace be with you."27 Then he said to Thomas, "Put your finger

Thomas is not present

John 20:24-25

Comment
Where was Thomas when the others met the risen Christ? We do not know, because we are not told. When the other members of the Inner-Circle told Thomas they had seen the risen Christ he could not believe it. Being brutally honest Thomas said unless he could touch the scars of the nails and the wound in the side he would never be able to believe. This is why some say Thomas was a doubter.

Thomas believes

John 20:26-29

Comment
For eight long days the other members of the Inner-Circle could talk of nothing but having seen the risen Jesus. Oh how Thomas wished he could join

here, and see my hands; and put out your hand, and place it in my side; do not be faithless, but believing." 28 Thomas answered him, "My Lord and my God!" 29 Jesus said to him, "Have you believed because you have seen me? Blessed are those who have not seen and yet believe."

in their belief that Jesus was alive. Out of fear of being arrested themselves they still kept the doors locked. Suddenly and without notice Jesus was standing among them. He greeted them with the words, "Peace be with you." Then he invited Thomas to touch his wounds if that would help him believe.

All of Thomas' doubts and fears were put at rest when he laid his eyes upon the risen Jesus. Jesus' reference to those believing who have not seen him is graphic indeed for people of all subsequent generations.

Breakfast with Jesus by the Sea of Galilee

John 21:1-3
1 After this Jesus revealed himself again to the disciples by the Sea of Tibe'ri-as; and he revealed himself in this way. 2 Simon Peter, Thomas called the Twin, Nathan'a-el of Cana in Galilee, the sons of Zeb'edee, and two others of his disciples were together. 3 Simon Peter said to them, "I am going fishing." They said to him, "We will go with you." They went out and got into the boat; but that night they caught nothing.

Breakfast with Jesus by the Sea of Galilee

John 21:1-3

Comment
Seven of the eleven disciples were together on the banks of the Sea of Galilee. Peter announced that he, "was going fishing." The names of five of the disciples are given while two remain anonymous. Who are the other four? Where are they?

Peter's decision to go fishing was an indication he was on the verge of returning to the old way of life.

After fishing all night, they had nothing to show for their labors. This could be seen as symbolic of what their life would be like if they forsook their ministry for Jesus. This is the first mention of Nathaniel since early in John's Gospel.

Try the other side

John 21:4-8
4 Just as day was breaking, Jesus stood on the beach; yet the disciples did not know that it was Jesus. 5 Jesus said to them, "Children, have you any fish?" They answered him, "No." 6 He said to them, "Cast the net on the right side of the boat, and you will find some." So they cast it, and now they were not able to haul it in, for the quantity of fish. 7 That disciple whom Jesus loved said to Peter, "It is the Lord!" When Simon Peter heard that it was the Lord, he put on his clothes, for he was stripped for work, and sprang into the sea. 8 But the other disciples came in the boat, dragging the net full of fish, for they were not far from the land, but about a hundred yards off.

Try the other side

John 21:4-8

Comment
This is an amazing fish story. Jesus asked a question to which he already knew the answer. Telling them to throw their net on the other side of the boat was reminiscent of the earlier meeting on these shores when he told Peter to let down his nets. Peter reminded him they had fished all night and caught nothing. He was reluctant to try at that moment because the sun was already up. With a shrug of the shoulder he did as Jesus said. To everyone's amazement they had to have help bringing the net full of fish ashore. Jesus had smiled and said if you follow me I will make you fishers of men, (Mark 1:17; and Matt. 4:19). Jesus did not intend for them to return to their old way of life.

Later Christians read these stories as also having symbolic

meaning. The number of fish (exactly 153) was seen as an indication of the success that the Christian mission would have. The undamaged net was seen as the capability of the church to contain all who entered.

In a more practical mode we understand the counting of the 153 fish was recognition that they would be expected to pay the usual tax for taking fish from Herod Antipas' lake.

John the apostle referred to himself as, "That disciple whom Jesus loved." It is he who identified the person on the beach to Simon Peter. Always the man of action, Peter, put on his clothes and jumped into the sea and swam ashore. Fishermen did not work in their clothes, to do so would soil and ruin them.

Having breakfast together

John 21:9-14

9 When they got out on land, they saw a charcoal fire there, with fish lying on it, and bread. 10 Jesus said to them, "Bring some of the fish that you have just caught." 11 So Simon Peter went aboard and hauled the net ashore, full of large fish, a hundred and fifty-three of them; and although

Having breakfast together

John 21:9-14

Comment

Landing their boats with their huge catch, the disciples found that Jesus already had bread and fish on the fire. As in feeding the 5000, Jesus' ability to provide was again demonstrated. Jesus did not

there were so many, the net was not torn. 12 Jesus said to them, "Come and have breakfast." Now none of the disciples dared ask him, "Who are you?" They knew it was the Lord. 13 Jesus came and took the bread and gave it to them, and so with the fish. 14 This was now the third time that Jesus was revealed to the disciples after he was raised from the dead.

After breakfast

John 21:15-19
15 When they had finished breakfast, Jesus said to Simon Peter, "Simon, son of John, do you love me more than these?" He said to him, "Yes, Lord; you know that I love you." He said to him, "Feed my lambs." 16 A second time he said to him, "Simon, son of John, do you love me?" He said to him, "Yes, Lord; you know that I love you." He said to him, "Tend my sheep." 17 He said to him the third time, "Simon, son of John, do you love me?" Peter was grieved because he said to him the third time, "Do you love me?" And he said to him, "Lord, you know everything; you know that I love you." Jesus said to him, "Feed my sheep. 18 Truly, truly, I say to you, when you were young, you girded yourself and walked where you would; but when you

need the disciples' catch of fish for their breakfast.

According to John this is only the third time Jesus had appeared to his disciples since his Resurrection.

After breakfast

John 21:15-19

Comment

This meal became an occasion for Jesus to restore Peter. There is a significant parallel between the three confessions of love and the earlier threefold denial that we saw in John 18: 15-18, 25-27.

This almost ritual reenactment of the earlier failure, placed in context, is an expression of the Lord's forgiveness, and recommissioning of Peter for the task he was to perform.

Peter was to look after Jesus' flock, a meaningful image for the church of John's Gospel, (see John 10:1-18, this is the "I am the Door" passage). He is to nurture them with teaching and pastoral oversight.

are old, you will stretch out your hands, and another will gird you and carry you where you do not wish to go." 19 (This he said to show by what death he was to glorify God.) And after this he said to him, "Follow me."

Peter is also alerted that in his old age he would be able to live up to the boast he had made in his prime, (see John 13:36-38, Peter promises to lay down his life for Jesus, who responds "You will deny me three times before the cock crows") he would accept a martyr's death with courage, (John 21:18-19.) According to tradition he insisted on being crucified head down because he felt unworthy to die in the same manner as the Lord Jesus.

What about him?

John 21:20-23
20 Peter turned and saw following them the disciple whom Jesus loved, who had lain close to his breast at the supper and had said, "Lord, who is it that is going to betray you?" 21 When Peter saw him, he said to Jesus, "Lord, what about this man?" 22 Jesus said to him, "If it is my will that he remain until I come, what is that to you? Follow me!" 23 The saying spread abroad among the brethren that this disciple was not to die; yet Jesus did not say to him that he was not to die, but, "If it is my will that he remain until I come, what is that to you?"

What about him?

John 21:20-23

Comment
As Jesus and Peter walked together along the shoreline, John was not far behind. We can only wonder at his purpose for following Jesus and Peter. Clearly Peter is somewhat uncomfortable with his presence.

On the surface it would appear that Peter is asking, "What will be John's job in this new era?" Jesus' response was later interpreted by new converts to mean that John was not going to die. From our perspective in time, it is obvious that Jesus was not talking about his return to earth or the lifespan of either disciple.

We are not told what Jesus had in mind when he spoke. Perhaps it may be best understood that Jesus was saying, "That is not your concern. You are going to be fully occupied fulfilling the ministry to which I am calling you."

Strange words

Strange words

Mark 16:14-18

14 Afterward he appeared to the eleven themselves as they sat at table; and he upbraided them for their unbelief and hardness of heart, because they had not believed those who saw him after he had risen. 15 And he said to them, "Go into all the world and preach the gospel to the whole creation. 16 He who believes and is baptized will be saved; but he who does not believe will be condemned. 17 And these signs will accompany those who believe: in my name they will cast out demons; they will speak in new tongues; 18 they will pick up serpents, and if they drink any deadly thing, it will not hurt them; they will lay their hands on the sick, and they will recover."

Mark 16:14-18

Comment

These verses are among those under question by some scholars. It is obvious that the quotes here are inconsistent with the rest of the Gospels. We have seen many examples of Jesus' frustration and anger at people and situations, but never has he acted or spoken in the tone reflected in these verses. Across the years, some persons have seen his reference to serpents and drinking deadly things as being marks of true Christians. I personally can hardly imagine these words ever coming from Jesus' lips.

In the Galilee, once more

In the Galilee, once more

Matthew 28:16-20

16 Now the eleven disciples

Matthew 28:16-20

went to Galilee, to the mountain to which Jesus had directed them. [17] And when they saw him they worshiped him; but some doubted. [18] And Jesus came and said to them, "All authority in heaven and on earth has been given to me. [19] Go therefore and make disciples of all nations, baptizing them in the name of the Father and of the Son and of the Holy Spirit, [20] teaching them to observe all that I have commanded you; and lo, I am with you always, to the close of the age."

Comment

Matthew indicates some of the disciples still doubted Jesus' resurrection even after seeing him. Jesus does not chastise or criticize them for what they feel. He commissions the eleven to go forth with a great challenge, a challenge that still stands before his followers today.

The Ascension according to Mark

Mark 16:19-20
[19] So then the Lord Jesus, after he had spoken to them, was taken up into heaven, and sat down at the right hand of God. [20] And they went forth and preached everywhere, while the Lord worked with them and confirmed the message by the signs that attended it. Amen.

The Ascension according to Mark

Mark 16:19-20

Comment

We must bear in mind these verses are among those challenged by many authorities with respect to their authenticity.

This account written under Mark's name speaks of Jesus being taken up while they were on the banks of the Sea of Galilee after the breakfast together. From this point, the remaining members of the Inner-Circle went forth everywhere to fulfill the commission to preach the gospel to all the world.

Luke's account of the Ascension	*Luke's account of the Ascension*
Luke 24:50-53 50 Then he led them out as far as Bethany, and lifting up his hands he blessed them. 51 While he blessed them, he parted from them, and was carried up into heaven. 52 And they returned to Jerusalem with great joy, 53 and were continually in the temple blessing God.	**Luke 24:50-53** **Comment** Luke records an entirely different scene of Jesus' ascension. Jesus guided them out of the city along the Valley of the Kidron, up the Mount of Olives, through the garden of Gethsemane, across the peak and down the slope toward Bethany. Stopping before reaching the town of Bethany, Jesus gave his final farewell statement. Jesus then ascended out of their sight. Now they were without his physical presence. However, their reaction was not one of fear, discouragement, or despair. They returned joyfully worshiping and praising Jesus the Christ. These three responses are significant; Worship: they turned their attention away from themselves and their grief and onto Jesus and his mission. And returning, they sought out familiar surroundings and a base of support for the awesome task that lay before them. In doing this gladly, they became heartened by the awareness that

their commission was divinely inspired.

In going repeatedly to the Temple to praise God, they sought strength for the journey from both the community of faith and the Author of life.

John's closing comments

John 20:30-31;
John 21:24-25

John 20:30-31
[30] Now Jesus did many other signs in the presence of the disciples, which are not written in this book; [31] but these are written that you may believe that Jesus is the Christ, the Son of God, and that believing you may have life in his name.

John 21:24-25
[24] This is the disciple who is bearing witness to these things, and who has written these things; and we know that his testimony is true. [25] But there are also many other things which Jesus did; were every one of them to be written, I suppose that the world itself could not contain the books that would be written.

John's closing comments

John 20:30-31;
John 21:24-25

Comment
John gives a similar closing in both Chapter 20 and 21. Some have concluded this to mean that Chapter 21 is an addition by a separate author. We should remember that writing materials were very expensive in the day of John, and when one suddenly realized that he was not through, it would not be uncommon for him to simply keep writing until finished. There are many examples in the writing of the apostle Paul, where this has happened.

Reference

Chapter 1

Sunday before Holy Week

Divergence in the reporting

Six days before Passover
John 12:1-2

Meal number 1

Bethany

Mary anoints Jesus feet
John 12:3

Nard

Crowd gathers to Jesus and Lazarus
John 12:9-10

Four Days Later

Two days until Passover
Mark 14:1a; Matthew 26:6

Bethany and Simon the Leper,
Mark 14:3a; Matthew 26:6

Simon the Leper

The issue of "Unclean"

Healing the "Unclean"

Show yourself to the priest

Woman anoints Jesus' head
Mark 14:3b; Matthew 26:7

Angry reaction
>Mark 14:4-5; Matthew 26:8-9; John 12:4-6

Jesus defends the woman
>Mark 14:6-9; Matthew 26:10-13; John 12:7-8

Judas stalks away
>Mark 14:10-11; Matt. 26:14-16; Luke 22:3-6

Judas the Traitor

Plotting to kill Jesus and Lazarus
>Luke 22:1-2; Mark 14:1b-2; Matthew 26:3-5; John 12:11

The meals at Bethany

Chapter 2

Monday

Monday, Jesus enters Jerusalem, Bring the colt
>Mark 11:1-7; Matthew 21:1-7; Luke 19:28-35

Our Palm Sunday observance
>Mark 11:8-10; Matthew 21:8-11; Luke 19:36-40; John 12:12-19

Jesus wept over Jerusalem
>Luke 19:41-44

Jesus enters Jerusalem Differing accounts
>Mark 11:11; Matthew 21:12-13; Luke 19:45-46

Chapter 3

Tuesday

The Fig tree
   Mark 11:12-14; Matthew 21:18-19a

Luke has a similar story
   Luke 13:6-9

Cleansing the Temple
   Mark 11:15-19; Matthew 21:12-13; Luke 19:45-46

Is this the second telling of the same story?

Greeks are among the Pilgrims
   John 12:20-26

For this purpose I have come to this hour
   John 12:27-36 a

Many of the authorities believed in Him
   John 12:36b-43

I have come as light into the world
   John 12:44-50

Healed those who came to Him
   Matthew 21:14-17

Challenge to Jesus' authority
   Mark 11:27-33; Matthew 21:23-27; Luke 20:1-8

Parable of two sons
   Matthew 21:28-32

Absent Landlord
   Mark 12:1-9; Matthew 21:33-41; Luke 20:9-16

Stone rejected by the builder
   Mark 12:10-11; Matthew 21:42-45; Luke 20:17-18

Angry Response
        Mark 12:12; Matthew 21:45-46

Teaching daily
        Luke 19:47-48

Back to Mount of Olives
        Luke 21:37-38

Chapter 4

Wednesday - Morning

Wednesday Morning, First day of Unleavened Bread
        Mark 14:12-16; Matthew 26:17-19; Luke 22:7-13

The Fig tree has withered
        Mark 11:20-25; Matthew 21:19b-22

Resumes teaching in the Temple
        Matthew 22:1-14

Luke has a similar story

Pharisees asked, "When is the Kingdom of God coming?"
        Luke 17:20-21

Pharisees and Herodians team up to discredit Jesus
        Mark 12:13-17; Matthew 22:15-22; Luke 20:19-26

Sadducees try to discredit Jesus
        Mark 12:18-27; Matthew 22:23-33; Luke 20:27-40

Scribes try to discredit Jesus
        Mark 12:28-34; Matthew 22:34-40

Jesus says, "Woe unto you Scribes and Pharisees, hypocrites!"
        Matthew 23:13-15

Jesus blisters all the ranks of spiritual leadership

Blind guides
> Matthew 23:16-22

Swallow a camel
> Matthew 23:23-24

Whitewashed tombs
> Matthew 23:25-28

You brood of vipers
> Matthew 23:29-36

Jesus Laments for Jerusalem
> Matt. 23:37-39; Luke 13:31-35

Jesus quoted 2 Chronicles 24:20-21

Jesus faces them down
> Mark 12:35-40; Matthew 22:41-46; Luke 20:41-47

Moses' seat
> Matthew 23:1-12

Widow's two copper coins
> Mark 12:41-44; Luke 21:1-4

Chapter 5

Wednesday-Afternoon

Jesus leaves the Temple
> Mark 13:1-2; Matthew 24:1-2; Luke 21:5-6

Jesus speaks of the end times
> Mark 13:3-8; Matthew 24:3-8; Luke 21:7-11

Tribulation
>Mark 13:9-13; Matthew 24:9-14; Luke 21:12-19

When the persecutions did come

Desolating sacrilege
>Mark 13:14-23; Matthew 24:15-28; Luke 21:20-24

Jesus makes references from the book of Daniel

Luke clarifies the situation

After the Tribulation
>Mark 13:24-27; Matthew 24:29-31; Luke 21:25-28

Lesson from the Fig Tree
>Mark 13:28-31; Matthew 24:32-35; Luke 21:29-33

No one knows when
>Mark 13:32-37; Matthew 24:36-44; Luke 21:34-36

Remain faithful
>Matthew 24:45-51

Jesus spoke in parables
>Matthew 25:1-13

No explanation for the bridegroom's delay

The Talents
>Matthew 25:14-30

Remain vigilant
>Luke 12:35-48

This parable recorded in Luke contains a strong resemblance to Matthew

When Jesus returns
>Matthew 25:31-46

Chapter 6

Wednesday Evening-The Last Supper

Wednesday evening, The Last Supper
Mark 14:17; Matthew 26:20; Luke 22:14

Jesus' hour had come!
John 13:1

Judas Iscariot, Simon's son, will betray Jesus
John 13:2-11

What have I done?
John 13:12-16

I am telling you before hand
John 13:17-19

Whoever receives the Disciple, Receives Jesus and the Father
Matt. 10:40-42; Luke 10:16; John 13:20;

One of you will betray me
Mark 14:17-21; Matthew 26:20-25; Luke 22:14-16; 21-23;
John 13:21

Biblical References

Lord who will betray you?
John13:22-29

Triclinium

Judas departs
John 13:30

The Bread and the Cup
Mark 14:22-25; Matthew 26:26-29; Luke 22:17-20

Table talk turns into a dispute
Luke 22:24-30

What does it mean to be, "Glorified?"
John 13:31-35

Peter and the Crowing Rooster
John 13:36-38

Simon, Satan demanded you
Luke 22:31-38

Luke quotes the prophet Isaiah

John says Jesus delivered His Farewell address defined

Jesus' Farewell Address

Let your hearts not be troubled
John 14:1-7

Some think of Thomas as a doubter

Lord, show us the Father
John 14:8-11

Whatever you ask in my name
John 14:12-14

If you love me, you will keep my commandments
John 14:15-17

What are Jesus' commandments?

Because I live, you will live also
John 14:18-20

He who does not love me does not keep my words
John 14:21-24

These things I have spoken while I am still with you
John 14:25-31

I am the true vine
John 15:1-11

You are my friends if you do what I command you.
John 15:12-17

If the world hates you, know that it has hated me
John 15:18-27

The reference in verse 25 comes from Psalms 35:19-21

When their hour comes
John 16:1-11

Is there a contradiction in v. five?

The Holy Spirit will guide you into all truth
John 16:12-15

Verse fifteen is a clarification of verse fourteen

What does he mean by a little while?
John 16:16-24

No more riddles
John 16:25-33

Jesus Benediction
John 17:1-5

Holy Father, keep them in thy name
John 17:6-11

Keep them from the evil one
John 17:12-19

I pray for those who believe through their word
John 17:20-26

Chapter 7

Wednesday Night

Gethsemane

They sang a hymn
Mark 14:26a; Matthew 26:30a

Mount of Olives
Mark 14:26b; Matthew 26:30b; Luke 22:39

"You will all fall away"
Mark 14:27-31; Matthew 26:27-36

The Primary source

The Garden of Gethsemane
Mark 14:32a; Matthew 26:36a; Luke 22:40; John 18:1

Eight of you stay here
Mark 14:32b; Matthew 26:36b;

Jesus takes Peter, James, and John
Mark 14:33; Matthew 26:37; Luke 22:41

My soul is very sorrowful
Mark 14:34; Matthew 26:38

I do not want this cup
Mark 14:35-36; Matthew 26:39; Luke 22:42

Asleep First time
Mark 14:37; Matthew 26:40; Luke 22:45

Jesus mildly rebukes
Mark 14:38-39

Asleep the Second time
Mark 14: 40

Asleep the Third time
Mark 14:41-42; Matthew 26:41-46; Luke 22:46

The Arrest

Judas and the arrest
Mark 14:43-46; 48-50; Matthew 26:47-50; 53-56; Luke 22:47-48; 52-53; John 18:2-9

Peter uses his sword

Mark 14:47; Matthew 26:51-52; Luke 22:49-51;John 18:10-11

Witness runs away naked
Mark 14:50-52

The Religious Trial

Jesus is taken first to Annas
John 18:12-14

Annas sends Jesus to the High Priest, Caiaphas
John 18:19-24

Jesus is taken to the High Priest
Mark 14:53; Luke 22:54a

Peter followed
Mark 14:54; Luke 22:54b-55; John 18:15a

Unnamed disciple was know by the high priest
John 18:15b-16a

Peter in the courtyard
John 18:18

First Challenge
Mark 14:66-67; Matthew 26:69; Luke 22:56; John 18:17a

First Denial
Mark 14:68; Matthew 26:70; Luke 22:57; John 18:17b

Second Challenge
Mark 14:69; Matthew 26:71; Luke 22:58; John 18:25a-b

Second Denial
>   Mark 14:70a; Matthew 26:72; John 18:25c

Third Challenge
>   Mark 14:70b; Matthew 26:73; Luke 22:59; John 18:26

Third Denial
>   Mark 14:71; Matthew 26:74; Luke 22:60a; John 18:27

And the cock crowed
>   Mark 14:2; Matthew 26:74b-75; Luke 22:60b-62; John 18:27b

Unnamed disciple aids Peter's access to the court
>   John 18:16b

I believe

Witnesses give conflicting false testimony
>   Mark 14:55-65; Matthew 26:59-66

Let the abuse began
>   Mark 14:65; Matthew 26:67-68; Luke 22:63-65

Chapter 8

Thursday-Day of Trials

Very early Thursday morning
>   Mark 15:1a-b; Matthew 27:1; Luke 22:66a

Religious trial continues
>   Luke 22:66b-71

Judas repents and hangs himself
>   Matthew 27:3-10

Verse nine poses a significant problem

What do we know about Judas?

Jesus is taken to Pilate
>Mark 15:1c; Matthew 27:2; John 18:28a; Luke 23:1

The Political Trial Begins
>Mark 15:2; Matthew 27:11; Luke 23:3

The Jews did not enter the Praetorium
>John 18:28b-30

Pilate sees no reason to get involved
>John 18:31-32

More Accusations
>Mark 15:3-5; Matthew 27:12-14; Luke 23:2

Pilates' first verdict
>Luke 23:4-5

Jesus is a Galilean
>Luke 23:6-7

Pilate sends Jesus to Herod
>Luke 23:8-10

Jesus is beaten a second time
>Luke 23:11-12

Herod sends Jesus back to Pilate
>Luke 23:13-16

Pilate begins the second questioning of Jesus
>John 18:33-38a

Release one prisoner
>Mark 15:6-14; Matthew 27:15-23; Luke 23:18-25;John 18:38b-40

A petition was required

Pilate has Jesus scourged
>Mark 15:16-20

This is my personal position

Chapter 9

Friday-Day of Crucifixion

Personal Position

Pilate tries for the last time to release Jesus
      John 19:12-13

It was now approaching mid-day
      John 19:14-15a

The hours of the day in the Gospels related to our present day
calculation of time

Pilate washed his hands
      Matthew 27:24-25

Barabbas is released
      Mark 15:15a

Jesus delivered to be Crucified
      Mark 15:15b; Matthew 27:26b; Luke 23:25b; John 19:16

Simon of Cyre'ne
      Mark 15:21; Matthew 27:32; Luke 23:26; John 19:17a

Crowd follows
      Luke 23:27-31

Golgotha
      Mark 15:22; Matthew 27:33; Luke 23:33a; John 19:17b

Jesus offered wine mixed with myrrh
      Mark 15:23; Matthew 27:34

The Crucifixion
      Mark 15:24a; Matthew 27:35; Luke 23:33b; John 19:18a

The process of crucifixion

The Third Hour
    Mark 15:25

Pilates Inscription
    Mark 15:26; Matthew 27:37

Caiaphas Objected
    John 19:21-22

Two Robbers Crucified
    Mark 15:27; Matthew 27:38; Luke 23:32; John 19:18b

Dividing the garments
    Mark 15:24b; Matthew 27:35a-36; Luke 23:34b-35a;
    John 19:23b-24

The verbal abuse begins
    Mark 15:29-30; Matthew 27:39-40

Religious leaders ridicule Him
    Mark 15:31-32; Matthew 27:39-44; Luke 23:35b

Even the soldiers joined in
    Luke 23:36-38

Compassionate Concern
    Luke 23:34a

One Criminal harassed Jesus
    Luke 23:39-41

One Criminal Believed
    Luke 23:42

Request Granted
    Luke 23:43

Mary watched
    John 19:25-27

The sixth hour
    Mark 15:33; Matthew 27:45; Luke 23:44

The Ninth Hour
>Mark 15:34; Matthew 27:46

Is Jesus calling Elijah?
>Mark 15:35-36; Matthew 27:47-49; John 19:28-29

Jesus gives up His Spirit
>Mark 15:37; Matthew 27:50; Luke 23:46a; John 19:30

Torn Curtain
>Mark 15:38; Matthew 27:51a; Luke 23:45

Earthquake
>Matthew 27:51b-53

Centurion Believes
>Mark 15:39; Matthew 27:54; Luke 23:46b-48

Women looking on
>Mark 15:40-41; Matthew 27:55-56; Luke 23:49

Hasten their death
>John 19:31-37

During the agony of the crucifixion

Joseph of Arimathea
>Mark 15:42-47; Matthew 27:57-61; Luke 23:50-56a;
>John 19:38-42

Joseph was a rich man

Chapter 10

Saturday / Sabbath

Sabbath: day of rest Day of more plotting
Matthew 27:62-66; Luke 23:56b

Chapter 11

Sunday-Easter

What was this first Easter Sunday like?

Location and description of the Burial Tomb of Jesus

The Garden Tomb, Jerusalem

Day break
Mark 16:1-2; Matthew 28:1; Luke 24:1

The problem of the Stone
Mark 16:3

Problem Solved
Mark 16:4; Luke 24:2

How had this problem been solved?
Matthew 28:2

What about the Guards?
Matthew 28:4

They entered the tomb
Mark 16:5-6; Matthew 28:5-6; Luke 24:3-8

Angel orders
Mark 16:7-8

Quick departure
> Matthew 28:7-8

Meeting Jesus
> Matthew 28:9-10

The others do not believe them
> Luke 24:9-11

John's account varies from the others

John's Report
> John 20:1-2

The "napkin"

Mary mistakes Jesus for the gardener
> John 20:11-18

Mary Magdalene
> Mark 16:9-11

Guards report to the chief priest
> Matthew 28:11-15

On the road to Emmaus
> Mark 16:12-13; Luke 24:13-35

Jesus appears in the midst of them
> Luke 24:36-49

Jesus is unexpectedly there
> John 20:19-23

Chapter 12

Following the Resurrection / Before the Ascension

Thomas is not present
John 20:24-25

Thomas believes
John 20:26-29

Breakfast with Jesus by the Sea of Galilee
John 21:1-3

Try the other side
John 21:4-8

Having breakfast together
John 21:9-14

After breakfast
John 21:15-19

What about him?
John 21:20-23

Strange words
Mark 16:14-18

In the Galilee, once more
Matthew 28:16-20

The Ascension according to Mark
Mark 16:19-20

Luke's account of the Ascension
Luke 24:50-53

John's closing comments
John 20:30-31; John 21:24-25

Study Guide

Chapter 1

- Discuss the importance of the Sunday before Holy Week.

- How many meals at Bethany are we talking about?

- Who poured the costly ointment? Why way it so costly?

- What is implied by the term "Inner-circle?"

- Why were they plotting to kill Lazarus?

Chapter 2

- What day of the week did Jesus ride into Jerusalem on the colt?

- Why did he select a colt for his entry?

- According to Mark, what did Jesus do when he entered the Temple?

- Why did Jesus not remain in Jerusalem overnight?

Chapter 3

- What is the significance of Jesus and the fig tree?

- In what way did the Temple authorities challenge Jesus?

- Why were the Temple authorities so upset by Jesus' parables?

- What is the significance of the comments concerning the corner stone?

Chapter 4

- Discuss why more Gospel material is dedicated to this day than any other portion of the story of Jesus.

- Why is it of interest that the Pharisees and Herodians teamed up to discredit Jesus?

- Then the Sadducees attempted to discredit Jesus.

- The Scribes (Lawyers) were next to try.

- Discuss the blistering language Jesus used in responding to his critics saying, "Woe unto you Scribes and Pharisees, hypocrites blind guides who can swallow a camel before seeing what is right, whitewashed tombs, and a brood of vipers!"

Chapter 5

- What was different Wednesday afternoon as Jesus left the Temple and returned to the slopes of the Mount of Olives.

- What is your reaction to Jesus' telling them about the end times?

- Discuss the tribulation, what does it mean? When will it happen?

- Define and discuss the great desolating sacrilege that would come to Jerusalem.

- Why did Jesus challenge them to remain faithful?

- Who knew / knows when these things did / would come to be?

Chapter 6

- Discuss Jesus' return with the Inner-circle to the Essene quarter to celebrate his last Passover meal.

- What day of the week did this occur?

- What does it mean His hour had come!

- Consider our favorite paintings of the Last Supper, is it a correct depiction?

- Discuss the Triclinium.

- Did Judas leave before the passing of the bread and wine?

- Discuss Jesus' farewell address to these his closest friends.

Chapter 7

- Discuss "After singing a hymn" what was the hymn? Where did it come from?

- Discuss the route Jesus took after they left the Upper Room.

- Why did they go through the Kidron Valley to climb the slops of the Mount of Olives and make their way to the Garden of Gethsemane?

- Inside the garden Jesus ordered eight of the disciples to remain at a certain place, why?

- Discuss why the big three were invited to go further?

- Discuss Jesus' being deeply troubled and asking them to remain awake and pray.

- How many times did Jesus rise from his prayers to find them asleep?

The Arrest

- Discuss how Judas knew Jesus would be in the garden.

- Describe how you would have felt had you been on of the Inner-circle at that moment.

- Discuss what Jesus meant when he announced that the hour was upon them.

- Discuss Judas leading a contingent of armed men to arrest Jesus.

- What is the meaning of the "Kiss?"

The Religious Trial

- Where was Jesus taken first?

- Who was Annas?

- Who was the High Priest Annas sent Jesus to.

- Why did Peter follow at a distance?

- Was another disciple present too? If yes, who was he?

- Discuss the unnamed disciple having access to Jesus' interrogation.

- Peter could not go further than the courtyard, why?

- Who were the witnesses who testified against Jesus?

- What happened when the questioning ended?

Chapter 8

- Discuss why very early Thursday morning Jesus' religious trial continued.

- Why did Caiaphas need the death verdict to come from his arch enemy Pilate?

- Why did Judas hang himself after he learned Jesus was being sent to Pilate?

- Discuss what we really know about Judas.

- If the trial by Caiaphas was a religious trial what kind of trial would Pilate conduct?

- Why didn't the Jews enter the Praetorium?

- What was Pilate's first reaction to the idea of a trial?

- Who did the religious authorities to Pilate?

- Discuss the significance of Pilate learning that Jesus was a Galilean?

- Discuss Herod Antipas turning Jesus over to his guards who beat him and returned him to Pilate.

- What was Pilate's reaction?

Chapter 9

- Why did Pilate try once more to release Jesus?

- Discuss the hour comparison chart and the implications of the statement, "It was now approaching mid-day."

- What was Pilate's intent when he washed his hands and released Barabbas?

- Was this the first, second, or third scourging of Jesus before the crucifixion?

- Discuss Simon of Cyre'ne being compelled to carry Jesus' cross.

- Discuss the process of crucifying described.

- What do you know about the other two who were crucified at the same time?

- Who voiced the only compassionate voice that day?

- Discuss you feelings for Mary at this moment.

- Discuss the significance of the curtain in the Temple being split from top to bottom?

- Discuss the risk and cost of Joseph of Arimathea asking for and being granted permission to take Jesus and bury him.

Chapter 10

- Discuss the meaning of this day being a Sabbath, and Passover rolled into one.

- What were the various groups who had played a role in the drama of the Crucifixion the day doing?

Chapter 11

- What was this first Easter Sunday like?

- Discuss how the accounts of Mark, Matthew, and Luke differ from the account of John's.

- Discuss the Folded Napkin.

- Who tells us about the guards and their actions?

- Who gives us the account of the events on the road to Emmaus and what is its basic meaning?

Chapter 12

- During the first Easter day Jesus appeared to the Inner-Circle, how many times?

- Where was Thomas?

- With Jesus' time on earth rapidly coming to a close, was the Inner-Circle in danger of falling apart?

- Discuss the lakeside breakfast.

- Discuss the conversation between Jesus and Peter.

- Review and discuss the closing comments of the four Evangelists.

Intermedia Publishing Group

Publishing That Works For You

Do you need a speaker?

Do you want Earl David to speak to your group or event? Then contact Larry Davis at: (623) 337-8710 or email: ldavis@intermediapr.com or use the contact form at: www.intermediapr.com.

Whether you want to purchase bulk copies of *The 8 Days of Holy Week* or buy another book for a friend, get it now at: www.imprbooks.com.

If you have a book that you would like to publish, contact Terry Whalin, Publisher, at Intermedia Publishing Group, (623) 337-8710 or email: twhalin@intermediapub.com or use the contact form at: www.intermediapub.com.